12 S77051

D1829138

LONDON BOROUGH
OF
LEWISHAM
LIBRARY SERVICE

Title

BOOK STORE

Books or discs must be returned on or before the last date stamped on label or on card in book pocket. Books or discs can be renewed by telephone, letter or personal call unless required by another reader. After library hours use the Ansafone Service (01-698 7347). For hours of opening and charges see notices at the above branch, but note that all lending departments close on Wednesday and all libraries are closed on Sundays, Good Friday, Christmas Day, Bank Holidays and Saturdays prior to Bank Holidays.

8)3/

4

19. JUN 8

03

Stress in your Life

BY THE SAME AUTHOR:

Social Work ('Target for Careers')

Edwin Packer

Stress in your Life

J M Dent & Sons Ltd London

LEWISHAM LIBRARY SERVICE

	BRANCH	COPY
LBN.		
SBN. 0-460-04105-3	2	
CLASS NUMBER 616-85	CATEGORY	
BOOK-SELLER B-m	INVOICE DATE 18/9/74	
ACC. NUMBER S77051		

First published 1974
© Edwin Packer 1974

All rights reserved. No part of this publication may be reproduced, stored in a retrieval system, or transmitted, in any form or by any means, electronic, mechanical, photocopying, recording or otherwise, without the prior permission of J. M. Dent & Sons Ltd.

Made in Great Britain
at the Aldine Press · Letchworth · Herts
for J. M. DENT & SONS LTD
Aldine House · Albemarle Street · London

This book is set in 156 Garamond 10 point, 2 points leaded

ISBN 0 460 04105 3

Contents

Acknowledgments and Author's Note

Acknowledgments are due to the following for permission to summarize or to quote certain passages from the books mentioned: to Sarah Morris and publishers George Allen & Unwin Ltd in respect of *Grief and how to live with it*; to Z. F. Stypulkowski and publishers Thames & Hudson Ltd in respect of *Invitation to Moscow*; to Clarence D. Lee and publisher Charles C. Thomas, Springfield, Illinois in respect of *The Instrumental Detection of Deception*; to Sir William Sargant and publishers William Heinemann Ltd, Harper & Row, and the Greenwood Press in respect of *Battle for the Mind*; to Alexander Weissberg and publishers Hamish Hamilton in respect of *Conspiracy of Silence*; to Opinion Research Centre and the *Evening Standard*, London, in respect of the research into *Life in the Capital*; to the *Lancet* in respect of the letter published therein from Drs J. S. Pippard and P. S. Greaves; and to the *New Scientist* in respect of a short quotation on the future of cities. Attempts to get in touch with Dr Thomas Holmes, originator of the Recent Events Scale, had not been successful at the time of going to press and his indulgence is asked in respect to references to his work. Thanks are also due to Roche Products for making available copies of their Stress monographs that are now virtually unobtainable.

The case history given in Chapter 9 concerning 'Mrs Shelley' and the Housewives' Register was used some years ago in an article I wrote on Loneliness for *Twentieth Century Review*. The other case histories come from my experience when a Probation Officer and concern people who were clients of mind or who consulted me about their marital problems. Names and other details have been changed to avoid the possibility of recognition.

EDWIN PACKER

1 One Thing on Top of Another

Cliff had a charm of manner that made other people have confidence in him, and when he abused this gift he found himself charged with obtaining money by false pretences. As it was his first offence the magistrates placed him on probation for two years. Towards the end of the period he told me he intended to get married. 'We got a bit too fond of each other, you know, and she caught for one,' was his way of explaining the unwanted pregnancy. This was some time before abortion became available almost on demand. Marriage was still considered to be the proper way of dealing with such a situation.

It was not until a year later that I met the eighteen-year-old girl he had married. She came to see me because she thought, being her husband's former probation officer, I might still have some influence on him.

During the eighteen months she had known him, life had been one long string of happenings. Cliff was the first man with whom she had had intercourse. She had become pregnant almost at once. Her parents disliked Cliff and gave consent for the marriage only with great reluctance. Before, she had been on very good terms with her parents; now there were bitter arguments that terminated when her father became enraged or her mother began weeping. Instead of having a normal, happy wedding it had been undertaken against a background of parental sadness and with everyone knowing that the reason for it was to legitimize the unborn child.

A few weeks after the baby was born Cliff's wife's mother

died. The girl felt that in some way this death was attributable to her and her association with Cliff. Then Cliff had been dismissed from his job and, most recent of all, he had become involved with another woman.

That Cliff's wife should subsequently have contracted psoriasis was regarded as just another stroke of the bad luck that had dogged her ever since she first met her husband. Yet today, thanks to the research done by men like Dr Thomas Holmes, professor of psychiatry at the University of Washington in Seattle, it would be thought stiange if she had *not* become ill.

For what Dr Holmes and others engaged in research along similar lines have shown is that it is not only germs and viruses that cause disease. Equally, if not more important, is the individual's general environment, which includes not only how he lives and where but also what happens to him.

Working with psychologists, Dr Holmes perfected the Life-Change Units Scale that enables the extent of change in an individual's life style to be measured. In constructing the scale Holmes and his staff noted down all the events, happy or unhappy, that occur in the lifetime of the average adult: engagement; marriage; childbirth; divorce; death; promotion; dismissal; unemployment; changes in financial status; holidays; quarrels with relatives, neighbours, colleagues; changes of residence or occupation; retirement; events in the life of children or grandchildren; major purchases such as of a new car, house or boat; accidents involving medical treatment or police action; incidents involving loss of cash or property—all these and more were listed.

The researchers did not place a value on each event themselves. They left this to the general public. Thousands of people in America and Japan were asked to place the events in order of their 'impact-fulness'. Surprisingly it was found that there was agreement on the relative importance of the various events in spite of the differences of the two cultures. Those interviewed both in Eastern and Western civilizations held the same views, in the main, about which life changes made most impact on them. In making the assessment the members of the public were asked to consider marriage as having a midway mark of 50, and to relate other events to it by asking themselves: does coping with this event involve more or less adjustment than marriage, and would the readjustment take more or less time?

A 'weighting' based on the replies was then given to each event by Holmes, the most impact-making happening having the highest score attached to it and so on down the list. By general consent the death of a spouse is regarded as the most strongly-felt happening. To this Holmes and his team have allocated 100 points. Moving to a new house is rated 20 points, going on holiday 13.

This was how the Life-Change Units Scale looked when the research was completed:

Life event	*Mean value*
Death of spouse	100
Divorce	73
Marital separation	65
Jail term	63
Death of close family member	63
Personal injury or illness	53
Marriage	50
Fired at work	47
Marital reconciliation	45
Retirement	45
Change in health of family member	44
Pregnancy	40
Sex difficulties	39
Gain of new family member	39
Business readjustment	39
Change in financial state	38
Death of close friend	37
Change to different line of work	36
Change in number of arguments with spouse	35

Life event	*Mean value*
Mortgage over £10,000	31
Foreclosure of mortgage or loan	30
Change in responsibilities at work	29
Son or daughter leaving home	29
Trouble with in-laws	29
Outstanding personal achievement	28
Wife begins or stops work	26
Begin or end college	26
Change in living conditions	25
Revision of personal habits	24
Trouble with boss	23
Change in work hours or conditions	20
Change in residence	20
Change in college	20
Change in recreation	19
Change in church activities	19
Change in social activities	18
Mortgage or loan less than £10,000	17
Change in sleeping habits	16
Change in number of family get-togethers	15
Change in eating habits	15
Vacation	13
Christmas	12
Minor violations of the law	11

Verifying the accuracy of the scale then began. The thousands of American and Japanese citizens who had been asked to give a weighting to each event that had occurred in their lives were asked for details of their medical histories. What emerged from correlating the events with the medical histories was that anyone with a high life-change score for events that occurred within a year was almost certain to be ill during the year that followed. In other words the eventfulness or non-eventfulness of anyone's life is related to his state of health. Too many events crowded into a comparatively short period of a person's lifetime, that call for a big adjustment in coping with the resultant emotional upheaval, is one of the major causes of illness.

Not surprisingly these findings have been put to good use. From the unit scale a Schedule of Recent Events has been drawn up, and many groups of people all over the world have since completed it by marking those happenings which occurred during the previous twelve months.

In August 1967 three thousand men of three American cruisers were in San Diego harbour, the cruisers being at the start of a six-month tour of duty. Was it possible to predict which men would be ill on voyage? The men completed the schedule, and based on the information they gave they were put into high-risk and low-risk categories. A record was then kept of the health of the crews in the following six months. There was a clear-cut correlation between the men who had been put into the high-risk category as a result of their life-change experience and the amount of illness. The computerized results showed that the men who were in the top 10 per cent of life-change units (and who therefore had had to adjust to the most change during the preceding year) had suffered twice as much illness as those in the bottom 10 per cent, and the higher their score the more severe their illnesses in character.

Commander Ransom J. Arthur, head of the US Navy Medical Neuropsychiatric Research Unit at San Diego, who was in charge of the project, said afterwards: 'It is clear there is a connection between the body's defences and the demand for changes that society imposes. We are in a continuous dynamic equilibrium.... Various "noxious" elements, both internal and external, are always present, always seeking to explode into disease. For example, certain viruses live in the body and cause disease only when the defences of the body wear down. There may well be generalized body defence systems that prove inadequate to cope with the flood of demands for change that come pulsing through the nervous and endocrine systems.'

In other words the more complex life becomes—and every

day technological change makes life more complicated for the individual—the greater the risk to health. Using the Schedule of Recents Events, an average score for a six-month period for a low-risk of illness would be between 40 and 60 units. Although some individuals are able to cope better with change than others, anyone scoring above 60 units in a half-year or 120 in a full year might expect some illness—and certainly would if the year's score reached 150. It has been found that life events tend to come together in the three months before the ill health begins, and the ill health itself usually takes the form of a cluster of illnesses, some of which may be no more than a bad cold or a sore throat.

2 *Stress Response—the Friend Turned Foe*

What is a stress situation? If people tell you that they have been under a great deal of stress they mean that certain circumstances have put pressure on them, perhaps causing some degree of mental and physical ill health. You know quite well what they mean. These circumstances may be as diverse as the death of a mother, the threat of having a house compulsorily purchased for a so-called improvement scheme, an unhappy personal relationship or a very boring monotonous job. A person's ill health is only indirectly due to these things; it is directly due to that person's reaction to them.

This is worth repeating. It is your *response* to these events that decides whether or not you are under stress. The existence of stress depends on the interaction between you and your environment. And you, as an individual, differ from me in the genes you have inherited. You differ in your physical constitution, your emotional constitution and your intellectual constitution. So it is to be expected that your response to something in the environment will be different from my response.

If I had been born deaf, living on the perimeter of Heathrow Airport would not be a stressful situation to me. But it may be a stressful situation for someone like you with normal hearing. In time the noise may affect not only your hearing ability but also your emotional stability by making you more nervous, irritable and unable to concentrate.

Being under stress therefore means that the body is responding to a threat, and according to the make-up of the individual the stress response can be comparatively harmless or potentially dangerous.

The stress response was for tens of thousands of years a protective device of the body enabling it to adapt to danger. It has become inadequate and unsuitable in modern times only because of the great changes that have taken place in our social and economic circumstances. The body's response mechanism has remained unchanged while society, which Man has created, has changed rapidly. The body is geared to react instantly when danger threatens—what the biologists call the 'Fight or Flight' reaction. But the dangers for which the body is so prepared are chiefly those faced by Man the Hunter more than ten thousand years ago. Then the swift reaction to a threat was very necessary. Our primitive ancestors were constantly having to decide, according to the circumstances, whether to fight or flee. Whatever the decision, the body's response had prepared it for instant action.

What happens when we respond to stress

Just what are the changes that take place when we respond to such a threat in the environment? We are mobilized for action by a complicated system that manufactures and secretes hormones, including adrenalin and noradrenalin, in the adrenal, pituitary and thyroid glands. The stress situation, which is seen, heard or imagined, causes a warning to be flashed from the brain to alert the autonomic nervous system (that part of the nervous system over which we have no conscious control). This in turn releases very powerful hormones. Within a few seconds they are taken by the bloodstream to all parts of the body. Through their action the heart beats faster and the blood pressure rises. Blood is forced more quickly into the muscles in readiness for action. The blood vessels are widened to help the flow of oxygen and to allow waste products, which the impending action will produce, to be carried away quickly from the muscles. And in the sensitive digestive system the secretion of gastric juices is stimulated. The hormones sometimes act too on the muscles of the bladder and gut, closing the sphincter muscles so that we have no urge to urinate or defecate during the time of crisis.

When the stress situation is particularly threatening, and the body's response is therefore intense, modern man begins to look like his ancestor of long, long ago. His eyeballs retract so that he can see better; this gives him a wide-eyed appearance which may frighten the enemy. His nostrils widen to increase the flow of oxygen in the body. Drops of sweat shine on the skin and the colour of the face changes, becoming either redder or paler. In extreme cases of alarm—in the presence of the supernatural, for example—the hair stands on end as it does in some animals, making the individual even more frightening to the enemy.

Life has always involved facing up to stress in the environment, and meeting the stress situation has meant both resisting it and adapting to it. So where does the danger arise, if it has always been part of existence? The answer is to be found in the rapid changes in Man's environment that have taken place in the last few hundred years.

Processing the signals

All living things are continuously receiving signals from the outside world. In Man the neural cells of the brain make patterns of these commonplace stimuli, and compare all incoming messages from the senses with these patterns. If any of the messages do not fit one of the established patterns the brain sends out an alert. Thus it is that we can concentrate on reading a book while other members of the family are moving about the house. Our consciousness is not disturbed because the noise made by the family is familiar and matches the established patterns. No threat is present.

But a stranger's step in the hall, or the low murmur of an unknown voice, or a loud crash that is totally unexpected—these things would register as 'foreign' and the brain would cause an alert to be flashed into the consciousness.

What technological change has produced in many aspects of our lives today is an excessive amount of these unexpected happenings which, because they are excessive, become stress situations.

Danger – real and imagined

Since the Industrial Revolution started in the eighteenth century, the happenings that cause these stress situations have both vastly increased in number and grown in intensity. Yet today it is only in war, and on those rare occasions when self-defence is needed, that we are called upon to fight or flee. But the body does not restrict the secretion of the stress hormones to these comparatively rare occasions. On the contrary the powerful hormones are sent through the body, causing the heart to beat faster and the blood pressure to rise, every time we are frightened by a low-flying aircraft, every time we get into a heated argument, every time we feel frustrated, every time we read, see or hear anything that stirs up anger or alarm or fear.

The danger does not have to be actually present; just to imagine it is often sufficient to bring about these bodily changes. Watching a play, a film or a television programme is enough; any of these can stir the emotions. The hormones pour into the bloodstream when fear catches at the heart at the possibility of an unpleasant confrontation, or when awaiting news of crucial importance. The development in Man of foresight, of the power to anticipate what may happen, is a double-edged weapon. It may be protective in that it allows preparations to be made. It can also be injurious because of the stress response it sets up in the body.

We do not know enough as yet about the relationship between our mental and physical processes to be quite certain why it is that a thought in the mind can bring about bodily changes over which the individual has no conscious control. Yet we know that it does so; we are all aware of occasions when thought has an immediate effect on bodily action which consciously we are quite unable to control. Listening to a comedian tell a funny story causes the diaphragm in the body to move up and down in laughter without any conscious message being sent. A candidate for a job waiting to be interviewed thinks about the ordeal ahead and the thought makes him start to sweat. Some men get an erection just by looking at a beautiful girl and imagining having sexual intercourse with her.

As has been said, many incidents that bring about a stress response in our bodies cannot be dealt with today by either fighting or fleeing. If an outlet for action does exist, it is likely we shall be breaking the law if we take it. A bad driver gives your car a bump; you feel angry and want to swing a punch at him. Do so and you could be charged with assault. Even shouting a few words of abuse—and speech is better than no action at all—could land you in trouble. Nevertheless as far as the body is concerned this 'letting off steam' is a normal response. Without it the body is liable to suffer damage, particularly if stress situations are experienced repeatedly. And repeated they will be for anyone who lives in an urban area of an industrialized country.

What is the likely effect of having the glands pump out hormones which raise blood pressure and increase the amount of blood fats and other substances, when these liberated substances cannot be used up in action? Briefly, the unused substances so released by the hormones do harm to the body.

It is worth while pointing out here the difference between anger and anxiety. Anger is the response to a 'here and now' situation; anxiety is the vague dread that something may happen, a dread that is all too common in our society when the individual feels that events which affect his life are beyond his control. The threat of eviction, of compulsory purchase of his home for an airport extension or a new motorway, fear of becoming redundant, of contracting cancer or some other killer disease are a few of the sources of anxiety that bedevil people today.

When it is anxiety rather than anger which is felt, there is an increase in blood sugar and a rapid heart rate. The effect is the same: unused substances cause injury to the body.

The general adaptation syndrome

A lifelong study of the body's response to stress has been made by a Canadian, Dr Hans Selye. Due to his work we now know in considerable detail the bodily processes which occur when we are subjected to continuous stress. Selye named the body's response the General Adaptation Syndrome. It is made up of three phases. The first and most dramatic has already been described—the rapid secretion of powerful hormones which prepare the body to resist its attackers or to deal with a threat. This first phase of the body's response may be quite sufficient to meet and defeat the danger which threatens. As we cross the road the sight of a car bearing down on us sets up the alarm reaction. The hormones stimulate the muscles and we jump out of the car's way. The body's defences have been successful.

But if the stress is continuous, or nearly continuous, then the body settles down to the second phase of the General Adaptation Syndrome, a stage of long-term resistance. In terms of warfare, if the first phase has been a 'border incident' with the enemy attacking and being quickly repulsed, then the second phase can be likened to the trench warfare of World War I. The body adjusts itself to a more prolonged struggle, during which bodily equilibrium is achieved, the sort of stalemate that occurred so often in that war. It then remains for one of the antagonists to weaken and the battle is over.

In our industrialized urban society the forces at work which create stress in the environment are getting stronger, not weaker. All too often it is the individual who succumbs. Intermittent or continuous stress situations cause the body repeatedly to respond. This is the experience of those who work for years in monotonous spirit-destroying jobs, of those who are involved in unhappy personal relationships, of those who live in fear of some ever-present danger or who feel anxiety about some disaster they imagine is about to happen. These are examples of stress situations in response to which the individual can frequently find no course of action that will allow him to make use of the 'fight or flight' readiness of his body.

Breakdown

The third phase is reached when the body can no longer make an adequate response to this flow of stress situations. The equilibrium between threat and response is no longer maintained. Exhaustion sets in, and severe illness or even death may result.

The defeat of the individual is hastened if his body is not working well. The body's response to stress is not always of sufficient force to hold the enemy. Sometimes the reaction is too weak and a breakdown occurs quite quickly. Sometimes the response is too powerful, so that the neutralizing chemicals are unable to cope with the hormones in the bloodstream and muscles. These then do actual harm to the body. Dr Selye calls the damage done to the body by its own defences 'the diseases of adaptation'.

In a sense illness caused by stress situations is always due to the physical and mental processes of the individual. If he cannot endure the strain put on him by traffic noise and harassment, by the noise of the factory floor, by the boredom of his job, by a nagging spouse or boss, by the anxiety occasioned by the ever-rising cost of living, then physical or mental exhaustion sets in. His resistance to disease is weakened and he falls sick. Or his mind, to protect itself from overwhelming fear and anxiety, cuts itself off from reality and he becomes mentally ill. If neither of these things happens then one of the diseases of adaptation may get him, accompanying one of these other forms of breakdown. Does this seem a gloomy picture?

When stress produces achievement

It should be emphasized that we can tolerate a stress situation—tolerate, that is, the body's response to it—if the situation is an isolated one. Indeed a stress situation frequently produces the best in us provided that we are able to take positive action. The body's response gives us the energy to tackle the task with zest. The athlete keyed up for a race is an obvious example. The writer or journalist who has a deadline to meet, and has put off the dreaded moment when he must face the typewriter and produce the message, often writes well in his burst to get his copy in before the time limit expires.

But if the athlete or writer has domestic or financial worries that provide additional stress situations to which the body's metabolism has already responded, he will not be in tip-top condition. Demands have already been made on him, so he is not keyed up totally for the job in hand.

The sensitive intestines

One part of the body which has told us more about our reaction to stress than any other is the gastro-intestinal tract, probably the most sensitive of the systems of the body and one that shows the greatest reaction when the body is under pressure. This fact has been known for many years. As far back as the 1830s an American army surgeon, William Beaumont, had working for him in his laboratory a technician named Alexis St Martin. The technician had received a gunshot wound in his stomach, which had failed to heal. He therefore had a gastric fistula (opening) that permitted not only the stomach lining to be seen but also allowed a flow of gastric juices to pass direct to the exterior. A plug kept the opening closed when experiments were not in progress.

On one occasion Beaumont carried out a rather unkind hoax on Martin. He told the man he was dismissed from the job. Not unnaturally the technician's feelings were of anxiety and anger. He felt sure that he would not be able to get other work with his stomach wound still unhealed. And he considered his dismissal to be unjust. The effect of these feelings on the stomach was such that the pink lining changed first to red and then to mauve as it became engorged with blood. Had there been a gastric ulcer there, undoubtedly it would have bled profusely.

Confirmation of these findings came in the present century from two doctors, Stewart G. Wolf, Junior, and Harold G. Wolff, working at Cornell University Medical College. They studied the response of a man with a similar fistula. When the man was involved in situations which gave rise to feelings of aggression and anxiety, his gastric secretions increased and the folds of his stomach lining became congested with blood.

Still further proof of the link between the stress response and the stomach was forthcoming from the medical records of some two thousand American young men who developed peptic ulcers as part of their response to military life. A check revealed that all had shown some emotional disturbance, 'butterflies in the stomach', under examination when first drafted into the Army.

Monkeys under stress

These findings have been corroborated on a number of occasions by experiments carried out on monkeys kept specially for medical research. Largely as a result of work done at the Walter Reed Army Institute of Research in America it is now known that ulcers are more likely to be caused not by continuous but by periodic emotional stress.

Monkeys used in experiments at the Institute were harnessed in pairs to chairs and worked a six-hours-on, six-hours-off schedule. During the 'on' periods, slight electric shocks were felt by the monkeys unless one of them (the 'executive' monkey) pressed a lever that cut off the current. The other monkey could also operate a lever, but pressing it had no effect. Monkeys learn quickly. The executive monkey soon recognized that he was the one who could prevent the shocks by pressing his lever. The other learnt that his lever was a dummy, and he only pressed it spasmodically. The six-hour period was found to be crucial, after a number of experiments had been made with other times. The six-hours-on was followed by six hours with the current cut off. While the executive monkey was hard at work pressing the lever to prevent himself and his fellow from being subjected to shock, the acidity in his stomach increased very little—for the action he was taking had effect. Yet at the end of the six-hour period during which time no shock had been experienced there was a great increase in stomach acidity. It would seem that the gastro-intestinal system has a rhythm of its own; in these experimental monkeys the cycle was a six-hourly one.

After twenty-three days of this rota the executive monkey died. Autopsy showed a large perforation in the wall of the duodenum, the site where ulcers often occur in humans. The other monkey, partner to the dead executive monkey, was still in good health. It was put to death. Autopsy revealed no gastro-intestinal abnormalities whatsoever.

The strain of decision-making on the executive monkey during these sessions, which were geared to coincide with the natural rhythm of his gastro-intestinal system, had brought about ulceration severe enough to cause death.

Ulceration of this tract is just one response which the body makes to stress situations. Ulcers are common in people who are constantly being exposed to stress situations at regular intervals. These people usually have to make decisions and accept responsibility. This alone is not enough, but where the pressure of the job has recently increased, or there has been additional pressure from some outside agent, then there is a strong possibility of peptic ulcers occurring.

When success spells breakdown

Dr Alexis Brook, consultant psychiatrist to the Tavistock Clinic and senior psychotherapy lecturer at St Bartholomew's Hospital, London, writing in *The Practitioner*, has emphasized the danger attendant upon success in management, particularly when a man reaches the peak of his ability and is promoted beyond that level. 'Over-promotion Stress' is the term applied by Dr Brook to this condition, which is not uncommon in the higher echelons of management. This is more fully dealt with in *The Peter Principle* by Laurence P. Peter and R. Hull.

First, there may be a long period when the promoted man is doing the new job inefficiently and succeeds only in making his subordinates feel frustrated. Then the stress situation produces a bodily response varying according to the individual. Three instances from the psychiatric records show typical stress responses to new responsibilities when the individual is promoted beyond his ability:

Mr A., a forty-three year old popular and energetic man, was promoted to manager—'a position which he had coveted'. Six months later he came to the doctor about his heart because he kept waking up at night with palpitations. 'Nothing to worry about,' he was told after a check-up. A year later he suffered a mental breakdown. He had become mentally ill because of the strains of his new job.

Mr B. was a technical specialist of thirty-five who did not have the personality to cope with the problems of handling a staff of twenty when he was over-promoted. He suffered panic attacks at work and asked the doctors for a few weeks off to recover.

Mr C. was one of the employees of Mr B. The whole department under their new boss had a lower morale and efficiency. Mr C. needed treatment for 'jittery' nerves, or chronic anxiety.

But not all decision-making men and women fall victims to peptic ulcers or anxiety or heart disease. It has been argued that illnesses such as peptic ulcers and heart attacks are not solely due to the body's response to stress situations but to Man's diet. In particular, heart disease, which kills two hundred thousand people in the United Kingdom every year, was thought to have been brought on by a diet high in saturated fats of animal origin that raise the cholesterol level in the blood. When the level is high, cholesterol deposits line the wall of blood vessels and in time block the flow of blood to the heart muscle.

But this theory leaves some questions unanswered. Why is it that certain primitive peoples—the Bantu, for example, in Africa—who eat a gross amount of animal fat, manage to enjoy almost complete freedom from heart attack?

According to American cardiologists the behaviour pattern of the individual is the decisive factor in causing heart attacks. Research done in 1968 involved the study of two groups of individuals who lived in the same community and ate similar amounts and types of animal fats in their diet. The active, aggressive group consisting of men who thrived on competition, who were highly time-and-deadline conscious, had six times as many heart attacks as the group of men who had easy-going, placid, relaxed dispositions.

In Britain more light has been shed on this situation by Dr Malcolm Carruthers doing research in chemical pathology. He found that there is a chain of biochemical events that link the aggressive stress response of 'competitive' men with the furring up of blood vessels with fatty material. In other words coronary thrombosis, the disease brought on by atheroma (the blocking up of blood vessels to the heart muscle) is a self-inflicted illness in people who make little effort to modify their response to stress situations.

This is underlined by the advice given to patients after a heart attack: to avoid competing in the rat race, to worry less, to take things easy. In other words to alter their way of life, to become relaxed instead of tense, competitive and aggressive.

The increase in secretion of adrenalin and noradrenalin is not limited to moments of crisis or high drama. Research in Britain and Sweden has shown that everyday events at work or in one's leisure time can produce the stress response. And as competitive, aggressive individuals produce more of these hormones than their easy-going colleagues, the danger of their contracting stress diseases such as peptic ulcers and heart disease is much greater.

But Man does not *have* to respond to all stress stituations by getting uptight and aggressive. Unlike the monkeys in the experiment (and all lower animals), Man is self-conscious. He has insight into his situation if he cares to use his intelligence.

There are some stress situations in which this insight helps to reduce the stress response. A man who normally reacts aggressively to criticism can tell himself to remain unruffled when criticism is voiced; he will need a change of attitude to accomplish self-control, but this can be practised. It is not so easy to remain relaxed when an air liner blankets all other sound as it passes over the rooftops, or as cars and lorries roar past down a busy road along which you are walking.

By trying to defuse the aggression we feel, and by becoming

more relaxed, we can reduce the stress response of our bodies. But urban living is today generating such a multitude of stress situations that it is impossible to avoid reacting to many of them. Consequently the danger is ever present of stress diseases developing or of a general lowering of the body's resistance to infection.

3 When the Mind Cries 'Enough!'

'I couldn't believe it was me behaving like that. But somehow I just couldn't help myself. I wasn't only snapping at the children. I'd scream and scream at them till I was blue in the face, and then I'd burst out crying. Once or twice the neighbours came round, wondering what was happening. What really upset the children was seeing me crying like that. They must have been terrified. And so was I. Then I'd hug them and tell them Mam had a headache and that Mam was sorry she shouted.'

This was how Mrs Morris described what she called her nervous breakdown. She and her husband had been to see me a year before about their failing marriage. When first married they had moved away from the slum area where both had been brought up. He had been an apprentice motor mechanic, but when his time was up he decided it was not what he wanted. He bought and sold second-hand cars and dabbled in scrap metal too. He got on well with the people he wished to influence because it paid him to do so. Underneath he was interested only in himself.

He was doing well enough to pay key money to get the tenancy of a house. His wife did everything he wanted. She submerged her personality to please him; the result was that he soon lost interest in her. I had the feeling that he only came to talk over his marital problems with the probation officer so that he could use it to his advantage later. You could almost hear him talking to friends and potential customers—'I did my best to make a go of it, even went to the probation officer to see if he could help.

But she was impossible to live with. You wouldn't believe some of the things she got up to.'

Within a few days of her husband leaving home, Mrs Morris heard that he had set up house with a married woman who had left her husband about the same time.

Individual response to stress

In some women, reaction to such a stress situation as the desertion of a husband would be physical illness. For others the mind would be affected first, and some would have both a physical ailment and a mental illness. It is impossible to predict which of the body's defences will give way, every individual being unique in the response he or she makes to a situation.

All wives would feel some emotional upset, because any out-of-the-ordinary event, happy or unhappy, is a stress situation. The overriding emotion at the departure of a husband could even be one of relief for a few women. Mrs Morris was not one of these. She had built her life around her husband and children. Instead of reproaching him for leaving her she tended to reproach herself. What had she done, or left undone, that could have brought about the separation? With this conflict going on inside her mind she had to cope with a much reduced standard of living—existing on the poverty line of social security payments those weeks when her husband failed to pay the court order for maintenance—and carry as well the sole responsibility for caring for the three children.

She was a strong, healthy woman, and her concern for her children helped her to keep going physically. But the mental conflict proved too great to bear. There was an indication in her history that her family had a predisposition to mental illness; one of her aunts had suffered for several years from severe depression.

Mrs Morris had two fears. First, she was afraid that when she had the screaming fits she would entirely lose control, would not be able to draw back from the outburst to comfort the children in their distress. 'I was terrified I might really let go one day,' she told me long afterwards. 'One Friday I had a throbbing head and I felt this uncontrollable shaking temper come over me. On the spur of the moment I ran round to a neighbour and asked her to keep an eye on the children for an hour while I went about a part-time job. In fact I went to the doctor's. Afterwards I told her where I'd been, and she used to look after the children for me when I went to the hospital.'

Her second fear was that on impulse she might injure her children. During the day, when she was busy in the house or out shopping, this dreadful thought would flash into her mind that she might pick up a knife and stab the children, or suffocate them as they slept. She tried to put it out of her mind, but, instead of lessening, the destructive thought became more and more frequent.

Fortunately the first consultation Mrs Morris had with the psychiatrist at the hospital (to whom her doctor referred her) led to action. The medical social worker at the hospital used her influence to get a home help into the Morris household, social security payments were increased and the co-operation of neighbours and relatives invoked. This support from various sources allowed Mrs Morris to remain at home while undergoing treatment for her illness instead of going into hospital.

Mrs Morris was in fact on the edge of breakdown; left without help she would undoubtedly have done something which would have disrupted the life of both herself and her children. Then she would have had to be removed from her normal environment. As it was, the routine of everyday life was altered. Although there was still the distress of being deserted by her husband, the pressure of looking after children on the near-starvation social security payments had been lessened by the intervention of the medical social worker. And there were now people willing to give her comfort and support.

How the mind reacts

When anyone becomes mentally ill as a result of stress situations there are broadly speaking two ways in which the mind demonstrates that it has had enough. One is through neurosis, the other through psychosis. The patient who develops a neurosis is still well in touch with reality. Mrs Morris knew that she was not acting normally when she had the screaming fits. She knew too that the obsession that she might kill the children was an indication she was unwell. She was alarmed at her symptoms. She could talk about these things to the doctor and psychiatrist, proof that she was in touch with reality.

But had she developed a psychosis she would have been almost completely out of touch with the real world. She might have become withdrawn, not speaking to anyone, or talking in a way that lacked coherence, using strange words that had a special meaning for her but for no one else. She might have alternated between periods of depression and high excitement. She might have heard voices or seen visions or believed that she was being persecuted. Then she would have had to be hospitalized.

There is seldom a single reason for mental breakdown. Analysis of the background history of patients shows that there are many stress situations acting as precipitating factors—broken love affairs, money troubles, marital difficulties, the onset of menopause, upsets at work or redundancy. And there can be experiences in the past, such as childhood or adolescent conflicts or war-time incidents.

With Mrs Morris it is likely that her husband's desertion brought deeper conflicts to the surface. Her father had died shortly after her marriage; she had suppressed her grief because she thought it would depress her husband and the children to have her weeping and moping about the house. It is possible that after this bereavement her husband became for her something of a father figure, and his desertion was thus even harder to bear. There could also have been hormonal changes brought on by pregnancy and childbirth.

In her case there was the sequence of stress situations which, ever since Dr Holmes's findings, we now come to expect will be followed by illness. The birth of the youngest child, her husband's desertion, the much-reduced circumstances in which she found herself, all these occurring within a year's span would have flashed a warning signal if Mrs Morris had ever been asked to complete Holmes's Schedule of Recent Events.

Phobias

Many stress situations give rise to a form of disability known as a phobia, which is an exaggerated fear of a particular object or happening. With some people this takes the form of a fear of a confined space (claustrophobia) or an abnormal fear of cancer (cancerophobia). Perhaps the most common is agoraphobia, the opposite of claustrophobia.

I first met this condition when I had a letter from a married woman, Mrs Simcox, asking me to call and see her. I replied suggesting that instead she called to see me. In her second letter she explained she never went out, for when she did so a feeling of panic swept over her.

The relationship between Mrs Simcox and her husband was worsening. He did not understand her fear of leaving home and thought it was an excuse for not going out with him. The shopping had to be done by neighbours or the Simcox children. The children suffered in a number of ways: they could never be taken anywhere by their mother, she did not visit their school and so earned a reputation for being unco-operative, and they witnessed frequent quarrels between their parents arising out of the situation.

Unfortunately for Mrs Simcox, she had a GP who was just as unsympathetic as her husband. But after I had a talk with Mr Simcox he was willing to try to help, even though he did not believe his wife's story of feelings of panic. He asked the GP to refer her to the psychiatrist at the hospital and he even paid for a taxi to take his wife to keep the appointment, and had time off from work to accompany her.

Later Mrs Simcox was sent to a London teaching hospital where what was then a new form of treatment helped her considerably, so that she could venture outside the house if a sympathetic person accompanied her. This treatment was desensitization, a method of removing a mental complex by getting the patient accustomed to the thing or object she dreads by gradual steps, first in the imagination and later in reality.

How 'Open Door' helps

In 1968 an organization called the Open Door came into existence to help agoraphobes to come to terms with their obsession. Formed by Mrs Alice Neville, herself once a sufferer from agoraphobia, the membership today is over three thousand.

The total number of agoraphobes in the country is estimated at one hundred thousand, of whom three-quarters are women. Of these, a questionnaire revealed, 5 per cent had never sought medical advice because of lack of understanding concerning the disability.

Not only does a stress situation contribute to the onset of phobias; lack of understanding and unsympathetic responses from near relatives, doctors and neighbours create still more stress, for the sufferer begins to think that there is nobody in the world who feels just as she does. One of the major benefits which membership of the Open Door gives is that it provides the agoraphobe with a sympathetic listener at the other end of the telephone or a recipient of letters. And every other month a newsletter of some ten to sixteen foolscap pages goes out.

It is not surprising that the principal activity of local branches, which now exist throughout the country, is to keep in touch with members by post and telephone.

Agoraphobes vary in what they can or cannot attempt. Some can make long coach journeys but cannot walk down the street to a bus. One woman can go a short distance to her child's school, but cannot face a visit to the supermarket. Another has forced herself to learn how to drive, but cannot undertake a car journey at a moment's notice; she must be prepared for it well in advance.

Young people are the most difficult to help. When the illness comes on they tell no one, but cut themselves off from their own age group by staying indoors.

What is psychotherapy?

When stress situations give rise to a neurosis—diagnosed in Mrs Morris's case as an obsessional neurosis—there are two ways of dealing with it. The patient's emotions of anxiety, hate or depression can be alleviated by physical means, using drugs or electric convulsant therapy (ECT). Or psychological methods known as psychotherapy can be employed. This involves a close examination of the patient's past and present way of life through discussion between him and the doctor.

Even treatment by physical means involves a certain degree of psychotherapy if the doctor-patient relationship is a good one. As every good doctor knows, the patient's faith in him is of considerable curative value. Just believing that a certain medicine will 'do the trick' is often sufficient to effect a cure, as is sometimes demonstrated when new drugs are being tested. Two groups of patients suffering from the same disease and matched in other ways by age, sex and the stage of development of the disease are asked to co-operate by taking the new drug. One group is given the drug; the other is given a substitute which looks the same but which is probably nothing more than a sugar pill. In some instances as many as 40 per cent of patients receiving the sugar pill have shown a distinct improvement, testifying to the power of suggestion.

A doctor who inspires confidence has a head start in the race for healing, but the doctor who lacks presence, who is unable to convey his interest in the patient's wellbeing, is at a disadvantage. The patient comes to him hoping for understanding. Illness often causes people to revert in their mental attitudes to those of their childhood, consequently they show a desire to be dependent on the doctor as they once were on their parents. The ability to use this dependence to help treat the patient plays a part in psychotherapy.

There is no agreed formula that psychotherapists follow. All that the various therapeutic methods share is the basic doctor-patient relationship built up during a series of interviews. The doctor looks at the situation that is currently creating anxiety in the patient and then tries to find the connection between it and similar situations in earlier life. Frequently there is a strong reluctance on the part of the patient to identify these tender spots in his emotional life. Hence the need for many interviews. The guilt feelings and anxieties of the patient are revealed by instalments as it were, and this is possible only when a strong bond has been forged between him and the psychotherapist.

During the course of the treatment the attitude of the patient towards the doctor is likely to undergo change. Starting off warily, the patient moves into a period of trust, and later may transfer to the doctor strong feelings of affection or dislike which he once felt for people in his past. He may even show signs of jealousy of other patients. As these feelings are explored the patient's self-understanding is increased, and in time the outward symptoms of stress disappear.

Psychotherapists do not pay overmuch attention to the actual symptoms displayed by their patients. They take Freud's view that the symptom—be it a series of debilitating headaches or a paralysed hand—represents the hidden conflict which the patient has unconsciously refused to recognize.

Freud and Breuer laid the foundations of psychotherapy by their method of psychoanalysis. Their work is still the basis of modern psychotherapeutic practice, although certain aspects of it have been modified in the light of experience.

Group therapy

One of the spin-offs from World War II was the introduction of group therapy. This was used to treat prisoners-of-war who had been repatriated. Twenty years before the prisoners of World War I had presented the War Office with a problem. On their return to Britain from German prisoner-of-war camps many were found to be guilt-ridden. They had strong feelings that they were to blame for being captured, and were full of anxiety both about their reception in Britain and their chances of finding employment.

To prevent a recurrence of this social problem at the end of World War II, the War Office established resettlement units and staffed them with psychotherapists. Group therapy was possible because the men formed a homogeneous group in that they all shared the same problem.

There are several forms of group therapy in use today. Some are 'directed'—that is, they have a leader who is acquainted with the background and problems of individual members. He is able to direct discussion towards common problems, such as that of the anxiety felt by a group of patients suffering from claustrophobia. The leader can bring into the discussion group members who, if left to themselves in a group without a leader, would say nothing.

Non-directed leaderless groups are usually limited to not more than ten members. They include the psychotherapist and the psychiatric social worker, although these two can be excluded if the group does not wish them to be present. The discussion enables the patients to reveal new facets of themselves to others in the group; they benefit from the insight into their problems by the others, and by the mutual support provided by the group.

The value of this method therefore lies in the feeling of acceptance by the group, which grows steadily with time. Man is born into a family group, and throughout most of his life—when at school, at work and often during his leisure—he is part of other groups. So it is not surprising that he can get help from a group of fellow sufferers when he submits to their criticism.

Selection of patients to take part in the groups is important. Some people have to be excluded. Psychopaths, for example, who rarely tell the truth about themselves (and frankness is essential to the successful working of a group) are excluded and so are hypomaniacs, who talk at great length, refusing to be hurried or deterred.

This form of psychotherapy is used today with various groups: offenders on probation from the courts, drug addicts, alcoholics, people suffering from anxiety states. All these have a similar problem. It has also been found useful with people who have no common problem. Encounter groups, now very much the vogue, are made up of people who join together for group psychotherapy in spite of tne fact tnat tney do not necessarily share a common problem.

Changing the environment

But psychotherapy by itself is not enough. There has to be some change in the patient's environment or way of life. With Mrs Morris the stress situation which triggered off her illness lay in the increased responsibility, coupled with a loss of support, which her husband's desertion brought about. There was an underlying conflict, which had remained dormant for a number of years, arising out of her relationship with her father. Psychotherapy brought this to the surface, and with the help of the psychiatrist Mrs Morris was able to resolve it. The medical social worker helped to lessen the pressure of everyday life on Mrs Morris of having to cope with her young family single-handed. Neither process would have effected a cure without the other.

Mental illness is increasing in urban societies where traditional beliefs and customs are breaking down, and technological change is introduced without sufficient regard being paid to its effect on people. Today a situation has been reached where mental illness is responsible for more absence from work than accidents or colds and influenza. In the year ended June 1971, working days lost due to mental illness reached 38.5 million compared with 28.5 million from accidents and 10.1 million from colds and influenza.

These facts brought forth a comment from David Ennals, director of the MIND campaign of the National Association for Mental Health: 'It seems almost beyond belief that mental ill health, a cause of lost working days far higher than strikes, should have such a low priority in government thinking.'

One woman in six and one man in nine spend some part of their lives in hospital receiving psychiatric treatment. The mental hospitals contain two-fifths of all hospital beds, and logically one would have thought they would also command about two-fifths of the current hospital expenditure. Not so. Such is the low priority given to mental illness by British governments that in 1970–1 mental hospitals received *less than one-fifth* of the total expenditure. A similar disparity applies to staffing. Only 11 per cent of all consultants are psychiatrists and only 22 per cent of all full-time nurses work in psychiatric hospitals.

4 *Diseases Linked with Stress*

Although it occasionally happens that illness developing as a result of the body's stress response takes both a physical and a mental form, it is far more likely that one will present itself to the exclusion of the other. Often physical illness clears up when mental illness develops. In general the physical health of patients who are mentally ill is much better than that of the public at large. An investigation in 1936, comparing the cause of death of patients in psychiatric hospitals with those in the community outside, showed that deaths from angina pectoris and coronary sclerosis in the community were thirteen to fifteen times more frequent than in psychiatric hospitals, goitre nine times, nephritis three times and cancer four times.

Research has shown that certain illnesses are likely to be caused by the influence of the emotions on the body. And there are other illnesses not due directly to the body's response to stress situations that nevertheless are aggravated or made to recur by emotional upset.

Work done, particularly in America by Dr Harold G. Wolff, investigating the *type* of person who falls victim to the complaints listed shows that they are linked not only by sharing the disease but often by their mental make-up. Migraine sufferers have been noted as hard-working, conscientious people. Peptic ulcer sufferers are recognized as great worriers both over the work they have to do themselves and the way work they delegate is being carried out. Yet they are prone to take on more and more responsibility, while at the same time feeling they are not getting the support they need from superiors at work or wives at home. Heart disease victims are usually full of vigour, driving themselves and subordinates to get things done swiftly and efficiently.

One very interesting investigation into the link between disease and mental make-up was published in the American *Journal of Chronic Diseases* under the intriguing title 'Why do wives with rheumatoid arthritis have husbands with peptic ulcers?' The research quoted showed that such marriages contained a great deal of open and repressed hostility between the partners. This derived from the expectations each had of the other at the time of marriage which had not been fulfilled, and that this hostility was a causative factor in the two diseases.

Again it should be repeated what Dr Hans Selye, the world's acknowledged authority on stress, has so often emphasized—that we do not all have the same capacity to withstand stress situations. He likens the energy each one of us can summon up to cope with stress situations to an oil well. Not all oil wells contain the same amount of fuel, and once that fuel has been used up it cannot be replaced. When it is gone the individual ages quickly and soon dies.

So there are two variables which affect all of us. We all differ in the hereditary capacity we have to withstand stress situations, and we do not all live under the same conditions or follow the same occupations. A man with good energy resources who chooses a career full of stress situations and who works in a city may break down in health *before* a man with fewer resources who follows an undemanding career in a rural area. Selye sums it up in the comment: 'There are two ages, one of which is chronological, an absolute, and the other which is biologic and is your effective age. It is astonishing how the two can differ.'

The way we live now therefore determines our life span. A man with a chronological age of sixty could have a biologic age of forty and could live to be a hundred. Or he could have a biologic age of eighty and be dead by the time he is sixty-one.

It is only in recent years that we have come to realize that we can choose which man we shall be, that the way in which we allow society to develop and the place we choose for ourselves in it, or allow ourselves to be pushed into, is indeed a matter of life or death.

Illness and the emotions

Some of the diseases which may have a link with stress situations for some patients are listed here. But if stress reduces the body's powers of resistance, even a slight cold becomes a stress illness.

Acne. This skin condition, common in adolescence, can be aggravated by a strong emotion, usually depression, generated by stress situations. When this happens, and an anti-depressant is prescribed to counteract the emotional upset, the acne will lessen in intensity—indicating the part played by the emotions.

Alcoholism. If not a disease, alcoholism is a serious health hazard. Alcoholics do not conform to a personality type, but in many the cause of the addiction is undoubtedly the protection which alcohol gives against anxiety. It allays depression and serves to bolster up the ego, relieves loneliness and gets rid of tension. So the researchers have found common factors in the background history of alcoholics, such as conflicts in childhood and the great need for affection and approval, which if not met leads later to reliance on alcohol. The comradeship and the feeling of solidarity that war work produced among civilians in World War II significantly reduced the incidence of both alcoholism and suicide.

Allergic Rhinitis (Hay Fever). This condition is generally considered to be a reaction to pollen or fur. Some psychiatrists believe that although it is not itself psychogenic, that is, it does not have an emotional origin rather than an organic basis, nevertheless its onset in certain individuals is part of a response they make to stress. For these sufferers the prospect of an unwelcome experience ahead brings on the hay fever. In such circumstances the condition can be regarded as a protection against any unwelcome experience which faces the sufferer in the near future. Either it prevents the individual from facing up to the situation (as he is not well enough to keep the appointment) or it provides him with an excuse, if he does face up to it, for failing to give a good account of himself.

Alopecia Areata (*Hair loss*). In this disorder there is loss of hair on one or more circular patches of the scalp. In some families the condition is hereditary but its occurrence is triggered off by emotional disturbance, such as a serious accident or shock. Influenza, acute fever or syphilis can also act as a precipitator. The condition clears up when the complaint triggering it off is successfully treated. A regrowth of hair—sometimes of a lighter shade—follows weeks or even months later. When alopecia is part of the body's response to a stress situation the loss of hair does not usually show itself until some time after the distressful experience.

Anorexia Nervosa (*Obsessive slimming*). Pressures created by society cause stress situations for the female teenager. Her body matures earlier than that of girls in previous generations. She is pressurized by the media to be slim, well-dressed, beautiful, intelligent and to have boy friends. Often, however, while appearing physically mature she is mentally still a child.

Anorexia nervosa is one frightening and baffling disease seen in teenage girls which often stems from these stress situations. In this condition a girl starves herself, and her menstrual periods cease. Mentally she is confused, and obsessed with a desire to lose even more weight. There is continual conflict as she fights against her body's clamour to eat; in particular it longs for sweet, starchy foods.

Although doctors do not as yet completely understand the condition, it is usually found that the basic problem is one of growing up. Most women face the emotional hurdles presented at adolescence and get over them. To some girls these hurdles are insurmountable and they try to retreat into a childlike state. The result is the onset of anorexia nervosa.

It often takes months or even years for parents to recognize this illness, from which, it is now estimated, as many as two in every hundred schoolgirls suffer in one form or another. It is extremely difficult to get such girls to consult their doctor, since the last thing in the world they want is to be treated.

Even when weighing as little as five stone, a girl with anorexia nervosa remains convinced that she is too fat and must lose more weight. The methods by which she achieves this can only be described as bizarre. Typically the family begin to notice that the girl no longer eats with them. She refuses to do so, claiming she is not hungry or has eaten beforehand. If she is forced to eat there are horrendous scenes.

Although it may appear that the victim has a complete aversion to food, the opposite is true. She is obsessed by food. Thoughts of it haunt her every waking minute, but she fears that if she indulges in so much as a morsel she will start swelling and will be unable to control herself. She will sublimate her lust for food by reading recipe books, cooking for others and watching them eat, all the while assured of her own self-control.

Sometimes anorexia nervosa may cease quite suddenly after a few months. In other cases it takes an even stronger hold and bizarre behaviour increases. The girl exercises her emaciated body mercilessly in an attempt to burn up any calories she consumes. She begins to give in to her secret longings for food and has gorging sessions in which she consumes vast amounts of it. The guilt she experiences after one of these is tremendous, and she may make herself vomit or take massive doses of laxative to prevent any weight gain.

If she is accused of behaving in this way she will fervently deny it and will make every effort to appear healthy and cheerful. However, there are even further tell-tale signs—her miseries are added to by cold, blue extremities and exhaustion from starvation.

Her life will continue to be a living hell of deceit until help is given. This is usually in the form of psychiatric treatment. Conflict with parents may underlie the disease in some cases; the girl has feelings of guilt stemming from her upbringing and sex education (or lack of it) and her sexual experiences with boy friends. There is an unconscious longing to get back to the time before sexual maturity, when such conflicts and consequent guilt feelings did not arise. But this is *not* the underlying cause in all sufferers; there are many theories as to the cause of the condition but all treatments involve re-feeding and psychotherapy.

The fear of normal adolescent weight is often found to be related to sexual problems, and it is usually the psychiatrist who helps the girl to realize this. Isolation from family and boy friends is often essential for complete recovery.

Asthma. Although this condition is an allergy, that is to say it is an abnormal reaction to substances that are generally harmless, psychogenic factors often provoke asthmatic attacks. So children with asthma do not conform to a clear-cut pattern; in many circumstances there are psychogenic causes and in others none at all. Some researchers claim that the mother-child relationship is of importance. They say the child feels deprived of maternal love and the asthma attack is a means of preventing him from being separated from her. Other investigators contend that mothers of asthmatic children are rigid, insecure and domineering. Still more say that the child feels his mother's love is conditional upon his coming up to her expectations in regard to behaviour or schoolwork or some activity like ballet dancing or playing an instrument, the mother being extremely ambitious for her child. In such cases the child is exposed to the possibility of failure which carries a double penalty, the loss of achievement and the loss of his mother's approval. The question still has to be answered: Why does the stress response take the form of asthma? Generally in such children before the asthma develops there has already been some form of respiratory dysfunction so that the breathing apparatus—mouth, throat and chest—is vulnerable to infection. Psychotherapy may be useful where emotional upsets cause the attacks. A lessening of pressure from the mother, plus the encouragement given to the child to become more independent of his mother and to find ways of self-expression, all help to alleviate the condition.

Cancer of the lung. In spite of the fact that the connection between cancer of the lung and smoking has been established, some investigators claim there is also a psychogenic element in its causation. Firstly, the addiction to cigarettes by some smokers is so strong that it cannot be broken, and this is in itself a psychogenic factor. There is a theory that the lung cancer sufferer conforms to a type that does not display strong emotion when he feels it, but 'assimilates' it internally. Severe emotional shocks in childhood or in later life are assimilated into the body instead of being expressed in the normal way by showing anger, fear or distress.

Conversion hysteria (Physical manifestation of an emotional conflict). This condition could well have been included in the preceding chapter on mental ill health, but it is given here because it shows itself as a physical disability. Physical symptoms such as a paralysed arm or leg successfully protect the patient from a situation that he fears. The mind imposes its will on the body knowing that if a certain situation is entered into (for example, armed combat) the mind will crack under the strain. A physical reason for preventing the situation from developing is therefore created, the individual himself having no conscious control over the process.

During both world wars some soldiers who greatly feared a return to combat duties became temporarily paralysed in the arms or legs, although no physical damage was present. They were not shamming; they were convinced they could not use the paralysed limbs. In some cases of conversion hysteria the skin becomes insensitive to pain so that pricking with a needle evokes no response.

Constipation. When a person does not have a bowel action at his normal regular interval he is said to be constipated. So the condition varies according to the individual. Healthy people may have only one bowel movement every four days and, provided this is regular, it cannot be regarded as constipation. On the other hand a person who defecates twice a day would be constipated if he went four days without a bowel movement.

The condition can be caused by intestinal tumours, metabolic disorders, diseases of the rectum and colon, and by stress. The stress arises in early childhood when toilet training starts and a parent scolds or punishes the child instead of showing gentleness and encouragement. Such treatment makes the child reluctant to sit on the pot or lavatory seat. Showing too much concern or anxiety about bowel movement produces over-anxiety in the child as well. Any training has failed which leads the child to associate the pot or lavatory with unpleasantness. Toilet training then becomes a stressful situation for him. He will avoid the whole business as far as possible and constipation is a probable outcome.

Children usually manage to become toilet trained in their own time without outside help. Some parents are not prepared to wait for this.

Dermatitis (Inflammation of the skin). Emotional disturbance, particularly extreme anxiety, has been shown to be a factor in this condition, coupled with a response to an allergy. The sufferers tend to be diffident individuals, unable to show aggression and quickly withdrawing from personal relationships that promise to become hurtful to their egos.

Dyspepsia (Indigestion). When the process of digestion is not working smoothly we are made aware of the fact in a number of ways—flatulence, heartburn, vomiting or nausea. Another name for any or all of these is dyspepsia. The term nervous or organic dyspepsia is given to the condition that does not arise from physical causes. Organic dyspepsia shows itself in loss of weight and quite intense pain in addition to the symptoms already mentioned. It can be indicative of such serious ailments as peptic ulcer, gastritis and cancer.

There is another condition known as functional dyspepsia which is not usually attended by loss of weight or intense pain. It is not easy to trace the causes of functional dyspepsia, but emotional upsets can be one of them. Such upsets affect the blood flow of the gastro-intestinal tract and stimulate the secretion of gastric juices in the stomach even if they are not required for the process of digestion. The excessive acidity in the stomach thus produces dyspepsia. Badly prepared or unsuitable food can be to blame. Eating too heartily can be another cause, or pregnancy in its early stages.

Enuresis (Lack of bladder control). The age at which children attain bladder control varies with the individual. One child becomes dry at night by the time he is three years old, another may not achieve it until he is six or seven. About 15 per cent of children still wet the bed when they are five, the figure decreasing with age. Some 6 per cent are enuretic at eleven years. For some children no cause is ever found. The disability in others can be attributed either to organic or to emotional factors. Those cases in which the emotional upset can be traced are far more numerous than those of organic origins. Abnormalities of the nervous system or the urinary tract or bladder which are present at birth account for some sufferers in the organic group. Inflammation of the bladder (cystitis) can also be a cause, the bed-wetting starting as the disease develops, and disappearing when a cure has been effected.

Any experience which causes emotional upset can delay the control which the child acquires with age. For a young child, going into hospital or the death of a near relative is such an experience. Anxiety concerning school or a disturbing parent-child relationship that creates stress—these too tend to prolong the bed-wetting habit beyond normal limits.

Some parents never seek advice, hoping that time will bring a cure. Help from the family doctor or the school's psychological service should be sought if the habit persists after the fifth year. Anti-depressive drugs have proved of benefit in some instances; the alarm apparatus which wakes the child at the first sign of wetting has proved effective in others.

Fainting. This is the most frequent cause of loss of consciousness, but it should not be confused with the loss of consciousness which accompanies epilepsy, catalepsy and some strokes. The common fainting bout is associated with a drop in blood pressure which in turn reduces the circulation of blood to the veins and increases the amount of blood in the blood-vessels of the abdomen. Simple fainting of this kind is often brought on by being in a stuffy overcrowded room or by a variety of sudden emotional shocks in which the individual experiences disgust, surprise, unpleasantness, a distressing sight or the sharp pain of an injection. All of these either alone or in combination can result in fainting. On collapsing on the floor, the accumulation of blood in the abdominal cavity responds to the force of gravity and flows back through the heart to the brain, restoring consciousness.

Another form, known as hysterical fainting, is a symptom of emotional upset. It afflicts young women who are free from anxiety, the fainting being brought on by mass excitement as is experienced when a crowd of girls are in the presence of a pop idol. This is one example of how an episode of intense and sudden happiness can nevertheless be a stressful situation.

Heart disease. There is a cleavage of opinion in the medical profession concerning the relative importance of certain risk factors in heart disease. Many doctors believe that high blood-pressure, glucose level, serum uric acid, cholesterol and smoking are chiefly responsible for the condition. Others say that these factors are important in only about a quarter of the cases, and that the patient's personality and the conditions under which he works—the responsibility he carries, the stress situations he encounters—are the main factors. The sufferer from heart disease is recognized as sharing similar characteristics with other sufferers from the disease. In other words they conform to a type—ambitious and full of energy to achieve higher and still higher goals. It is to be expected that this type wins promotion and so takes on both a greater work load and more subordinates to control. Stress situations increase in proportion.

Urban living has grown in complexity and intensity this century and rapid change is making more and more demands on man's adaptability. This process is accelerating with a corresponding increase in stress situations. The incidence of heart disease has also accelerated. It was comparatively rare in the 1920s; nowadays it is the major cause of death in people under the age of sixty-five, claiming more victims than cancer, accidents, pneumonia, influenza or suicide.

Migraine. The cause of this condition is unknown. In many sufferers the bouts of nausea, vomiting and blinding headache that occur can be anticipated, for often there are precipitating factors. For some, lying in bed late at the week-ends or eating a particular food may bring on an attack. For others the migraine acts as a warning not to do too much. Migraine sufferers are usually of the type who are over-conscientious, methodical, hardworking. So the warning signs often appear *before* an important occasion for which the individual has been working for several days, weeks or months—an end-of-term concert, a wedding in the family, even a much needed holiday. Obviously, then, a psychosomatic mechanism is involved. Dr M. Critchley, who reported on his research into migraine in the *British Medical Journal* in 1950, concluded that the complaint represented 'an inborn type of reaction to a number of stresses both psychological and physical.'

Organ neuroses. There are situations in which an emotional conflict between love and hate leads to the hate being repressed. This sometimes happens in childhood when a child is dominated by his parents to the extent that he is unable to assert himself. He feels guilty that he should resent his parents so much and his resentment is suppressed. Although lacking an outward manifestation the suppressed hostility is still present, creating tension in the individual. It can take a physical form such as muscle contractions or heart palpitations. So the patient with an organ neurosis will appear calm and unemotional, yet his body is displaying the physical signs that accompany anger.

One of the significant features of life in an industrialized society is the high incidence of stress situations in which the body's response is a liability, not an asset, and yet the body still reacts in the traditional manner. Many employees who fear dismissal, and who are subjected to constant criticism by those who have the power to dismiss, suppress their hostility. The 'fight or flight' response dare not be used. Outwardly meek and subservient, the anger shows itself in one of the organ neuroses—muscle contractions or palpitation.

Palpitation. In some people excitement, fear, anxiety or flatulence can cause palpitation, an irregular beating of the heart which makes the individual think it has missed a beat. Palpitation is brought about by a change in the stroke volume or the rate of heartbeats. The individual becomes aware of the irregularity, and the realization that his heart is not performing normally serves to increase the irregularity. It can also be a manifestation of organ neurosis (q.v.).

Peptic ulcer. This is a general term for all varieties of gastric and duodenal ulcers found in the digestive tract. The lining of the stomach consists of cells which produce gastric juices in the form of pepsin and hydrochloric acid. Between them these juices break down the food in the stomach in the process of digestion. Normally the secretion of pepsin and acid should occur only when food is present and then the process of digestion neutralizes the powerful gastric juices. If the individual is suffering from any form of stress, the anxiety and fear will stimulate the secretion of the gastric juices even when the stomach is empty, and so the neutralizing of the pepsin and hydrochloric acid does not take place.

This was proved, as mentioned in Chapter 2, by research done over a number of years on a Canadian trapper who was wounded in the stomach in a gun accident. He recovered, but was left with a hole in the abdomen. Through this hole doctors observed the changes in the interior of the stomach, and they were able to record the reaction to alcohol, food and emotion. It was established that strong emotion calls forth a response in the stomach, the gastric juices being secreted in spite of the absence of food.

Should there be a break in the stomach lining—if for example there is a small abrasion caused by food from an earlier meal not being properly chewed, the gastric juices will attack this spot. So the habit of taking hasty meals, 'grabbing a sandwich' because the job does not allow leisurely eating, is likely to produce ulcers if anxiety or fear are part of the life style of the individual.

Eating habits, temperament and heredity assume greater importance in the formation of gastric ulcers than they do in duodenals; it is known that the amount of stomach acid is actually diminished in patients suffering from gastric ulcers.

Constant or intermittent anxiety seems to accompany certain occupations. Business executives and doctors have the highest incidence rate of people suffering from peptic ulcers (10 per cent), foremen and forewomen are in second place (9 per cent) with farm workers (2 per cent) and draughtsmen (1 per cent) at the other end of the scale. In general, jobs that entail decision-making and responsibility are more likely to produce ulcers in job holders than work that is mainly physical.

It is not surprising, bearing in mind the part played by stress in peptic ulcer formation, that the patient is made to rest and so cuts himself off from the situation that is helping to cause the stress response. When the patient recovers, some modification of his life style is essential or the condition will recur.

Polycythemia. This is the condition in which there is an abnormally high number of red blood cells in the circulating blood. One cause is a heavy loss of fluid through prolonged vomiting, diarrhoea or sweating, all of which can be symptoms of stress. It is thought that one form of the disorder, Polycythemia Vera, is due to the body's response to stress stimulating the symptomatic nervous system. The resultant flow of adrenalin through the liver increases the rate of blood clotting, and in middle-aged and elderly people this clotting may bring on cerebral and cardiac thrombosis.

Post partum depression. Many mothers feel depressed after giving birth, although fortunately in most cases the depression is mild, so mild that they get over it without recourse to the doctor. At the other end of the scale are those mothers who experience a depression so severe that it may lead to attempts to kill the baby or to suicide or both. The depression, from which every year eighty-eight thousand women suffer, can arise from feelings of anxiety following the mother's realization that she is now responsible for the baby. There is anxiety in some instances brought on by the thought that she and her husband will no longer be so close, that the baby will separate them rather than bring them together. If this were not enough, some women have all kinds of guilt feelings about becoming a mother, and others have unconscious fears of the new situation to the extent that the mind tries to dissociate itself from reality. Severe depression is one way to accomplish this. Currently American psychiatrists are investigating a theory that giving birth produces a stress response akin to that seen in soldiers returning from combat or prison camps.

So the stress presented by the new situation can in a variety of ways affect the mental health of some mothers. Not all psychiatrists go along with these explanations of post partum depression, believing that hormonal changes in the body are responsible, or that the cause lies in the excitation of the limbic system of the brain. Psychotherapy and drugs such as imipramine are part of the treatment. For more severe cases there are mother-and-baby units at a few psychiatric hospitals where treatment is given. Not only is the mother allowed to have her baby with her, but her husband can live in the unit too. It is a comment on our society that, in spite of the success of these units, some have been closed. The alternative is the splitting up of the family; the mother goes into an ordinary ward of the psychiatric hospital, the father remains at home, the baby goes into local authority care.

Pruritus vulvae. This is an itching of the genital region, particularly affecting women. In some sufferers it accompanies an unsatisfactory sex life, and is often complementary to the stress arising from frustration or frigidity. The infection can be shared by both husband and wife. Because it is milder in men the husband often does not feel the need for treatment and consequently, even if his wife is successfully treated, he may re-infect her.

Psoriasis. This disease consists of the formation of silvery scales on the skin and nails: when the scales are removed, usually by the sufferer picking at them, blood oozes from a number of tiny points. The lesions are commonly found on the skin over the knees and elbows, on the scalp and eyebrows, behind the ears and in skin folds. There is a link between the condition and stress, although the connection has not been definitely established. It is known, however, that the number of people suffering some form of emotional disturbance who also suffer from psoriasis is much greater than the proportion of the general population that has the disease.

Stammering and Stuttering. These are interruptions in the normal flow of speech, the stammerer being very hesitant, and the stutterer repeating certain sounds before managing to give vent to the complete phrase. One cause is thought to be the failure of one cerebral hemisphere of the brain to dominate the other, which might explain why some sufferers are left-handed but have been made to use the right hand. The condition is also attributed to a disturbed parent-child relationship, or to a subconscious attempt to hide something shameful. In both these instances a stammer would be a form of neurosis.

There is some evidence of a connection between stammering in children and a very high standard demanded of them by strict parents. Speech therapy and psychotherapy have been proved to be of value in the treatment of this condition.

Tic. This is a sudden involuntary contraction which occurs in a muscle or group of muscles. It serves no useful purpose. Eye-blinking, shoulder-shrugging, head-shaking, cheek- or mouth-twitching are all common forms. Often a tic is associated with mental illness, particularly hysteria, although it must be emphasized that not all tics arise in this way.

A person who suffers from a tic displays the twitch more often when he is emotionally upset, showing the relationship between the affliction and stress. Some paediatricians believe that nervousness, tension and anxiety in some children are a factor in producing tics.

Ulcerative colitis. A serious form of inflammation of the large bowel or colon in which the symptoms are bloody diarrhoea, ulcerations and loss of weight. While there are probably no psychosomatic factors causing the condition, in some patients stress situations aggravate the disease or cause it to recur.

5 *Inescapable Stress Situations*

Stress situations can be separated under two headings—those derived from the environment (environmental stress) and those caused by personal relationships (social stress). In many situations both environmental and social stress situations are present. The case history of Mr Carmichael illustrates the interaction of environmental and social stresses.

Mr Carmichael worked in the forge of a steel works, and over the years the noise gradually made him deaf. He was unaware of this; when people mentioned he was getting hard of hearing he attributed it to wax in the ears. He found that his social life was affected, and in time he became less anxious to go out at night. His wife was dissatisfied. She took to going out with women friends, behaviour which made her husband slightly jealous.

Other details of the rift between them were discussed during interviews between the couple and the probation officer, discussions which took place at the request of the magistrates, who hoped that a separation could be prevented. The wife complained that not only did her husband no longer take her out but he did not talk to her in the home. In the early days of their marriage, when she was preparing the evening meal in the kitchen, she used to call through to him in the dining-room and they would hold a conversation, but in recent years he only grunted in reply to her comments. She took this as a sign that he was no longer interested in what she had to say. After the husband had been to his doctor, it was made clear that his apparent lack of interest arose from his inability to hear what she said.

Noise that produces a stress situation is an example of environmental stress. The deteriorating relationship between Mr and Mrs Carmichael is an example of social stress. In this instance they interacted, but most of this chapter will deal with stress in the environment.

The attitude of people towards hearing differs from that concerning sight. We act as though we do not believe that our hearing can be injured. If the harm done to hearing by the environment were to threaten our sight instead, there would be a great public outcry.

The body lags behind

We fail to realize that our sense of hearing is geared to man's environment of thousands of years ago. It is not only our bodily response to stress that is based on the needs of Man the Hunter; our hearing is too. And our environment has changed so drastically, especially in the past two hundred years, that our bodily mechanism has had no time, in evolutionary terms, to adjust. Consequently we still have the 'fight or flight' response to stress which we no longer need, and we have a delicate hearing system which has not adapted to the ear-shattering impact of urban Man. We lack the protection necessary in the high noise environment we have created. If we wish to preserve our sense of hearing we shall have to reduce the noise in the environment.

Our sense of hearing can adjust to intermittent noise. The mechanism of the inner ear is such that it needs time to recover from fatigue after it has been bombarded by loud noise. But for anyone who is exposed to noise without respite, possibly not from one source only but from several, the process of recovery and restoration of hearing does not take place, and so permanent damage is done, as happened to the steel worker.

Research has shown just how much the urban environment has reduced our sense of hearing. A few years ago American scientists visited the villages of the Mabaans, south of Khartoum. The Mabaans did not use guns or drums; spears were their weapons and lyres their martial musical instruments. Checking the noise level in the villages, the researchers found that it was about the same as that in the reading-room of a public library. The hearing of the villagers was measured and compared to that of a group of Americans who had *not* been exposed to continuous noise. The hearing of male Mabaans aged between seventy and seventy-nine was better than that of the Americans aged between thirty and thirty-nine.

Noise levels are measured in decibels. Up to 50 decibels the environment is positively peaceful. Normal conversation takes the noise threshold up to 60, and if you are walking along a road and a lorry driving at forty miles an hour comes past, the noise level goes up to 84 decibels, imposing a strain on the hearing from which the ear needs time to recover. On a busy road no such opportunity occurs, and the cumulative effect is certain to do damage to the hearing. By building near to motorways, or constructing motorways through residential districts without rehousing the inhabitants on either side, society inflicts physical injury on some of its members. It does the same to those living on the perimeter of airports.

Even in the home noise is increasing. A dishwasher registers 75 decibels, a food-mixer 88, a washing-machine 78. With two of these labour-saving appliances switched on at the same time the body is under stress and likely to suffer permanent damage if the situation is often repeated. Should anyone in the house work in a noisy environment, or be subjected to high noise levels getting to and from work, he is unlikely to escape injury to his sense of hearing.

Deafness in factory workers

Research done by G. K. Keatinge and S. Laner on noise levels in British factories revealed that some riveters, working in conditions where maximum noise levels ranged from 115 to 128 decibels, suffered a hearing loss of more than 15 per cent after being exposed to those conditions for a year, and a loss of 38 per cent after five years. As all the men concerned were under forty years of age, the factory noise was making them old before their time.

An American study at the Carnegie-Mellon University showed that between five and fourteen million workers in the United States suffer hearing damage as a result of work noise. Eight million workers are exposed to noise above 95 decibels or more. The Environmental Protection Agency estimates that noise levels in certain parts of America have risen so high that the hearing of forty million people is at risk.

There is a growing body of evidence that excessive noise affects not only the hearing. The response to stress made by the body is so acute that actual organic change takes place, which displays itself in what are now recognized as stress diseases. Work done by Dr Gerd Jansen in Germany showed that workers continuously exposed to a noise threshold of 90 to 95 decibels frequently had a high diastolic blood pressure. This is the pressure in the brachial artery during the resting phase of the cardiac cycle, and is the lowest pressure—on average between 70 and 90 for a young adult. Other studies showed that continuous exposure to noise levels of 75 decibels can cause the blood vessels to constrict, resulting in permanently high blood-pressure. Newcomers to the work environment at first recover from its effects; when they return home in the evening their blood-pressure returns to normal. But after a period in the same employment there is no longer this return to the norm; blood-pressure remains high both at work and away from it. According to Professor William Burns of London's Charing Cross Hospital, when Man is exposed to the highest levels of noise, general symptoms such as giddiness, nausea and excessive fatigue may occur.

Although it is not always sound to draw a parallel between animals and Man, studies with laboratory animals have shown that the level of blood cholesterol increases if animals are exposed to continuous noise. And the higher the amount of blood cholesterol the more likely is it that the supply of blood to the heart muscle will be reduced, causing heart attacks, through atheroma, a condition in which a fatty, porridge-like substance is deposited in patches in the inner and middle layers of the coat of the larger arteries. When the animals used in the experiment were pregnant females a 20 per cent increase in birth defects occurred.

Education suffers

Teachers in schools situated in noisy areas, especially those in the vicinity of main roads, motorways and airports, experience greater difficulty in teaching pupils to read and to communicate than in schools in quieter districts. Dr James Miller, a consultant to the American Environmental Protection Agency, asserts that the development of speech and reading skills in young children is retarded if there is a constant noise level of 70 decibels. This is below the accepted safety level of 80 decibels for intermittent noise. The damage is done at this lower level by the absence of a recuperative period, which cannot occur because the noise is continuous. It is a feature of stress that isolated stress responses by the body do no harm. Repetition, continuity, a succession of stress situations calling forth bodily responses one after another, are what do the damage.

It is no coincidence that a survey of people affected by the noise of Heathrow Airport revealed that the number admitted to hospital for mental disturbances was eight times the national average. In a debate on noise in the House of Lords in March 1973 Lord Sandford, Under-Secretary of State for the Environment, admitted that two million people were 'annoyed' by the noise of Heathrow Airport.

Noise pollution

Efforts to reduce noise near airports are of course commendable, but much of the emphasis has been on spreading the noise pollution more thinly and not on reducing the total amount. Only about £1 million is spent yearly on quietening aircraft engines—a pitiful amount when considered alongside the £800 million spent on the Concorde project, which will greatly add to environmental stress. There is a tendency for governments to assume that aircraft noise is a problem only around airports, but country-dwellers more than fifty miles from Heathrow are also sufferers.

In order to lessen noise around Heathrow, pilots climbing out of the airport have instructions to throttle back so as to observe the 'zone of minimum noise' that extends from ten to fifteen miles. But once out of the zone and over open country they open up the engines. Consequently the full blast of aircraft noise is felt by country-dwellers over a large area before the aircraft reaches the coast. And the duration of the noise pollution is longer because the engines are allowed to reach their peak slowly.

At Richmond, Surrey, jets roar overhead from or to Heathrow one at a time in a minute-by-minute procession. But when summer holiday flights are at their most frequent, hitherto quiet rural areas on the Hampshire-Surrey-Sussex borders have to endure the roar of three jets overhead at the same time, either bound for or leaving Heathrow, Gatwick and Luton.

It has taken much public protest over the years to make governments aware of stress situations in the environment.

How little authority considered the wellbeing of the individual is shown by the existence of a statute that became law in 1920 and took away from citizens the Common Law right to sue when aircraft noise became excessive. It was thought that if anyone could sue—and win—then civil aviation in Britain would have no future.

As far as aircraft noise is concerned the stress response it generates is certain to intensify, for the British Airports Authority estimates that the number of aircraft movements will increase from 306,000 in 1970 to 660,000 in 1990. Soon there will be no such thing as 'quiet' in south-east England.

A recent report on aircraft noise has disclosed that in one town in the south-east about forty miles from Heathrow the number of quarrels between married couples has increased, especially at week-ends, because stress situations created by aircraft noise have led to irritability and frayed nerves.

Governments have a bad record in their efforts to reduce the noise levels of the environment. Not unnaturally, industrialists are unlikely to take action against noise unless compelled by statute to do so, for noise reduction is an expensive business. In particular, traffic noise has been steadily increasing over the years. Even the regulations that do exist to control it are all too rarely enforced.

Traffic noise ignored

A survey carried out by the Consumers' Association and published in its magazine *Motoring Which?* showed that the 1969 regulations on maximum decibel levels were not being enforced. The association calls for suitable test sites and the use of decibel meters. Although *Motoring Which?* found many suitable sites, the police argued that it was a lack of such sites and a lack of manpower that prevented them from enforcing the regulations.

The Consumers' Association carried out its own roadside tests; within the area of operations 7 out of 3,500 vehicles were clearly violating the noise regulations, giving an estimated 20,000 violations for the country as a whole.

Some ten years ago a government committee of inquiry recommended that vehicles which exceeded 85 decibels should be made illegal. This recommendation was ignored as far as lorries were concerned, and the Motor Vehicles (Construction and Use) Regulations of 1969 allowed lorries to reach 89 decibels. As *Motoring Which?* reported, these regulations were never strictly enforced. In August 1973 the Department for the Environment announced that Britain has been forced by the EEC to accept noisier standards still for lorries—no less than 91 decibels. Matters are made worse by the fact that since 1963 there has been a fivefold increase in the number of lorries on the road. Regulations, of course, apply only to individual vehicles and not to the overall noise, which can well exceed the limits for cars or lorries.

The car defeats the railways

The country's economy operates to increase rather than reduce motoring stress. To help the car industry no limit has been set on the number of cars produced. Attempts so far to reduce overcrowding on the roads have been feeble in the extreme—a few bus lanes in London, and in some cities a ban on heavy lorries using the roads through the city centre, but in London the ban is frequently ignored. There are many partial solutions that have never been tried, for example, insistence that private motorists use their cars only on certain days of the week. Railways, no longer profit-making, had their services severely cut back after the publication of the Beeching Report in 1963, thereby forcing more people to look to road transport to get about. Here is Mr Eldon Griffiths, Under-Secretary of State for the Department of the Environment, talking, as it happened, at a bus operators' dinner in September 1972: 'We are pro-bus only because the bus can preserve civilized life in our towns and in the countryside.' And a few days later he had this to say: 'It is the motorcar which offers the greatest hope to rural areas, provided that it is shared more freely.'

For political reasons—road transport and road-building being profit-producing, whereas the rail system has to be subsidized—there was no mention, you notice, that closed railway branch lines should be reopened. The increase in road traffic as a direct result of railway closures has led to a clamour for more motorways, with the inevitable destruction of thousands of houses. Yet because the railways do not make a profit their social advanages are ignored.

Motorway construction produces environmental stress, filling the vicinity with noise and dirt not just for a few days but for many months. Destroying houses produces social stress—anxiety about rehousing, about finding new jobs, about the means of travelling to existing employment, about the rental of the new house or flat. And those who do not have their homes destroyed endure environmental stress while the motorway is under construction and later when it is operating.

Environmental stress from road works and road traffic is likely to increase in the future. The motorway 'box' around

London is one possible future cause of stress situations, although the GLC Labour victory in 1973 has postponed the project. Another was indicated in the 'leak' to the *Sunday Times* in October 1972. But for this disclosure the public would have been kept in ignorance up to the very last minute of the Ministry of Transport's plans to reduce still further the country's railway network. The Blue Book outlining proposals suggested that British Rail's 11,600-mile network be cut to 7,000 miles in an effort to make the rail system economically viable. This would entail the abolition of 120 grant-aided passenger services outside London.

Large areas of Scotland, Cumberland, Lincolnshire, East Anglia, central Wales and the west of England would be left without rail services. Scores of stations would close and many rail employees would become unemployed. The report envisaged the transfer of 62 million tons of rail freight to the roads. To carry such freight heavy lorries would have to travel an additional 450 million miles on the roads. A simpler way of grasping the situation is to remember that it takes fifty heavy lorries to transport the coal carried by one coal train.

Money values triumphant

The report admitted that the environment would suffer, that road accidents and unemployment would increase, but presumably all this has to be borne to provide a commercial solution to the running of the rail system. The positive contribution that a rail system makes to the health of the community is ignored by such proposals. A steadily increasing subsidy (estimated at £40 million in 1972) seems small in comparison to the advantages gained by the community, for the rail system is extremely safe and does little harm to the environment. Governments are supposed to balance the interests of all sections of the community. The present transport policy looks at everything in financial terms and ignores the increase in stress situations for the general public.

Even without the suggested cuts in rail services, which would force 250,000 more people to travel on the roads every day, the stress situations from road traffic will certainly increase. Every year 17,000 more heavy freight vehicles go on the road; during the years 1961 to 1971 there was a 60 per cent increase in road freight.

Now entry into the European Economic Community has forced Britain to accept a much higher weight limit for lorries than was formerly imposed. Before she entered the EEC the Community had already decided on an axle-weight of 11 tons. Think of the shaking that a weight of 11 tons on each of four axles can do to nearby buildings as such a lorry passes. In Britain the limit had been 32 tons total weight.

The cost of allowing the 44-tonners into the country has been estimated at between £150 and £200 million per year for road-works alone.

This takes no account of damage to buildings, increased noise, and of stress situations for pedestrians and other road-users. It ignores the difference between Continental roads and those in Britain. On the Continent the main roads are straight, and the houses situated well back. British main roads twist and turn and run through town centres and residential areas where houses are only a few feet away from the road. Yet to meet the demands of European big business the British Government imposes on its people these stress situations that can only result in ill health for many who are exposed to them. Commercial values take precedence over human values.

Chemical smog

Just what our big cities may very soon experience has been clearly stated. At the annual meeting of the Chemical Society and the Royal Institute of Chemistry in March 1973 Dr R. G. Derwent of the Warren Spring Laboratory, Stevenage, Hertfordshire, said that an analysis of air pollution from traffic showed that formation of chemical smog similar to that in foreign cities might be experienced in London. The smog was believed to have come from the chemical process in which unburnt hydrocarbons, nitrous oxides, carbon monoxide and other products from the petrol engine can be processed by the action of the ultra-violet rays in sunlight.

Already in America a situation has been reached where clean air standards are impossible to achieve unless car traffic is reduced by 82 per cent. A series of public hearings in southern California early in 1973 convinced Federal air pollution officials that it will not be feasible to bring about a major reduction in car usage in the Los Angeles basin, where some ten million residents drive six million cars.

Instead the likelihood is that the Environmental Protection Agency will recommend a combination of less stringent measures that will include conversion of vehicles operated by fleet owners to natural gas fuel, improved public transport, car pooling and various 'disincentives' to driving cars into the major commercial areas.

Los Angeles is the first of thirty-seven metropolitan areas to be confronted with a Federal Government order to change transportation 'life-styles' to meet Federal air quality standards, which become effective in May 1975.

Local officials acknowledge that the proposed remedial steps, plus the introduction of exhaust-control devices on all new cars, will not produce clean air by that date.

The possibility of petrol rationing was raised during the hearings, but it was generally conceded that a large-scale reduction of car traffic would inordinately disrupt the area's economic and social life.

In London, faced by a deteriorating and stress-producing environment, the general feeling among its residents is one of helplessness. This was shown by the result of an investigation conducted for the *Evening Standard* by the Opinion Research Centre in April 1973; that feeling was shared by all classes. The report said:

'As for the quality of life in London there is scarcely any more optimism among the more affluent citizens—the young and middle-class voters—than there is among the rest about how the capital is shaping up to the future.

'QUESTION: Do you think London is becoming a better or a worse place to live in?

BY AGE

	All 1970 %	All now %	*Age* 18–24 %	25–44 %	45–64 %	65+ %
Better	20	12	13	16	8	11
Worse	56	73	72	68	79	74
Neither	18	13	15	14	11	14
Don't know	6	2	—	2	2	1

BY CLASS

	AB %	C1 %	C2 %	DE[1] %
Better	12	12	14	10
Worse	73	71	73	75
Neither	13	15	12	13
Don't know	2	2	1	2

'The new factors

'Perhaps one of the new factors in Londoners' attitudes to their environment is awareness and anxiety about pollution. Significantly more people show concern about fumes from traffic and factory smoke than in 1970—particularly the young. The young

[1] A, upper middle class (non-manual). B, middle class (non-manual). C1, lower middle class (non-manual). C2, skilled working class (manual). D, working class (manual). E, those on lowest level of subsistence (pensioners, handicapped, etc., manual and non-manual).

also show less than average concern about traffic noise, but are more likely to be bothered by crowded public transport.
'QUESTION: Which if any of these particularly bother you?

BY AGE

	All 1970	All now	*Age* 18–24	25–44	45–64	65+
	%	%	%	%	%	%
Traffic	42	46	46	54	47	29
Fumes	31	46	49	49	47	36
Traffic noise	29	31	21	27	37	35
Crowded transport	31	30	42	31	29	23
Smoke	9	17	31	20	11	8
Aircraft noise	12	16	11	15	18	18

BY CLASS

	AB	C1	C2	DE
	%	%	%	%
Traffic	61	47	45	37
Fumes	52	56	41	39
Traffic noise	39	34	27	27
Crowded transport	26	33	30	32
Smoke	12	17	20	16
Aircraft noise	16	16	15	17

'Man is only just beginning to realize that while engaged in conquering "natural" sources of environmental stress—extremes of temperature, drought and flood—he has created many more "unnatural" ones. Urban Man can no longer live a simple life. He has too many things to do, complex problems to solve, all related to his fragmented life in the city. In such a situation he looks back fondly to the past when life appeared to be more leisurely and much less aggressive, in comparison with a present which in Western civilization is geared to more and more industrialization and the stress situations it creates.'

The rapid growth of cities is a pointer to the amount of future environmental stress situations awaiting us and our children; the noise, the polluted atmosphere, the overcrowding, the difficulties in getting to and from work, the scarcity of housing, the rising level of crime. Crowding together also increases social stress situations, as well as those in which the environment and personal relationships interact to heighten still more the pressures on the individual.

According to the Institute of Science Hygiene at The Hague, urban population growth is about 6.5 per cent yearly—a rate which doubles the population of towns and cities every eleven years. This can be more readily appreciated when one realizes that just over a century ago, in 1850, there were only four cities in the world with a population of one million. In 1960 the number had risen to 141. A quotation from the *New Scientist* succinctly exposes the dangers of this rapid urbanization: 'The growth of cities is a major phenomenon in the world's development. But the enormous demand on technological goods and services created by vast populations gathered in urban groupings may in the long run be cripplingly expensive to the national economy as a whole. And in addition the quality of life in the cities may be eroded through the sheer bulk of humanity in which the individual is submerged.'

6 *Stress in the Overcrowded City*

The Phillips family, parents and five children, lived in the end house of a terrace off a main road. Traffic, particularly the Corporation buses that stopped near the terrace, made a continuous background of noise against which family life was conducted. Mr Phillips was a borderline mental defective, unable to do any but the simplest of jobs. His employment record was poor. The family was unpopular with neighbours, who made the Phillips children the scapegoats for any breakage, theft or disturbance. The house was damp. Paper would not stay on the walls; sink, drains and outside lavatory were frequently blocked. With two bedrooms to accommodate seven people, the baby slept in the same bed as the parents and the eldest girl slept downstairs on a couch. But other families in the terrace were just as overcrowded; nine out of the twelve houses held more than four occupants, so it was common for babies to sleep in the same bedroom as parents, for brothers and sisters of all ages to sleep in the same room and for eldest children or grandparents to sleep downstairs. Even so, these families were better off than the many homeless in the city.

Mrs Phillips kept the family together as best she could. She worked part time as an office cleaner. Often she went with her husband to the employment exchange to make sure he registered for work, and to urge the clerks behind the counter to find suitable work for him. At thirty-five she looked fifty, with hardly a tooth in her head and no money to pay even for National Health dentures.

The struggle finally exhausted her. Worn out by an inadequate husband, the cares of a large family, the wretched housing conditions, the incessant noise from the road outside, lack of sleep and quarrels with neighbours, she attempted suicide by putting her head in the gas oven.

It is a tribute to her that no major catastrophe had hit the family before, and the only social worker to visit the home had been the Education Welfare Officer, who made routine calls because of the non-attendance of the children on various occasions.

But now, after Mrs Phillips had been removed to hospital away from the environment in which stress situations had built up one on another over the years, social workers descended to help the family—as they had done to help Mrs Morris, the deserted wife whose case history was given in Chapter 3. The health department put pressure on the landlord to do essential repairs. An employer was found who was able to put Mr Phillips on the payroll in a simple sweeping job. Neighbours, feeling slightly guilty, offered to give what help they could. A home help came in to give a professional touch to the efforts of the Phillips's seventeen-year-old eldest girl, who had been no help to her mother before but who now took over the running of the household.

One stress on top of another

Both environmental and social stresses led to this breakdown. Mrs Phillips's relationship with her husband, the responsibilities she had to undertake which made her in effect the breadwinner and head of the family, the lack of sleep brought about by the youngest child's having to share the parental bedroom, the reluctance shown by the eldest children to help in the house, these were the sources of social stress. The slum house, overcrowding and the background noise of traffic provided the environmental stress situations.

It is only to be expected that experience of continuous stress situations is common among people living just on or below the poverty line. As has been shown in many studies of poverty and delinquency, these are usually the families with large numbers of children who live in the drab, decaying and overcrowded areas with inadequate playing space—the neighbourhoods, in fact, with greater unemployment, more mental and physical illness and a higher crime rate than anywhere else in the city.

It could be argued that Mrs Phillips's efforts to keep the family going without outside help had worked against its interests, for if social workers had been involved with the family at an earlier stage the support they could have given may have prevented the suicide attempt. Some pressure is taken out of a stress situation if the person under stress can talk to someone not directly involved. The experience of the Samaritans, founded in 1964 as a suicide-prevention agency, has shown that hundreds of lives can be saved yearly if someone willing to help can be reached any time of the day or night, but orthodox social workers cannot usually be contacted after office hours. In British towns with a twenty-four hour Samaritan service the suicide rates have tended to decline, while in towns in which the organization does not operate they have tended to rise.

The overcrowded rat colony

Observing animal behaviour patterns has given us insight into human behaviour. Laboratory experiments have shown that the degree to which an animal suffers from stress can be altered by changing his bodily reactions, making him more or less sensitive, or by administering drugs or by altering the amount of stimulation he gets by contact with other group members.

The experiments dealing with alterations in the amount of stimulation received from fellows in the group are important when considering Man's own living conditions. As far as he is concerned there is very much more social interaction now than in the past, so the possibility of conflict is increased unless we adopt new forms of behaviour.

One celebrated experiment has shown the effect on rats of stress situations caused by overcrowding. John Calhoun, an

American animal behaviourist, built a small colony to accommodate 80 domesticated albino rats. When the experiments started the number of rats totalled 48; a year later, in June 1958, it was 308. About the time when the third generation of rats had been weaned and were beginning to move about the colony, a change in behaviour from normal to abnormal was seen.

One of the changes had to do with nest building. When this was in operation rats of both sexes made several trips in quick succession to a pile of paper strips before going off to engage in some other activity. Both male and female rats built the nest, although the females did more of the work at a time just before they gave birth to the litter and immediately afterwards. The nests were well made of intermeshed strips, with a cup-like depression in the middle.

This normal nest-building behaviour became disrupted in September 1958 as overcrowding grew worse. Rats would pick up strips of paper to start the building process and then would abandon them to do something else, dropping the paper before the nest had been reached. Often the pile of paper strips remained untouched; no nest was built and the young were delivered on the bare floor.

The behaviour of mother rats in transporting the young also changed. Under normal circumstances when a female rat with a litter is disturbed (either by the intrusion of its nest by a strange rat or a human) the mother transports the entire litter to another place, and completes this task before engaging in any other activity. When overcrowding was rife the litters were often disturbed, and then the mothers started transporting the young to another place. But the stress of overcrowding had so affected these mothers that they failed to complete the transfer of the litter. Becoming distraught during the process, they went on to do something else. Then, going back to complete the transportation of the young, they forgot where they had deposited those already moved. At the end of the prolonged operation the young were scattered. When in an extreme state of disruption, the mothers would even take a baby out of the nest, move away and drop the baby on the floor. Baby rats so dealt with eventually died where they were dropped, and then were eaten by other rats.

Sexual behaviour disturbed

The sexual behaviour of the animals, particularly that of the males, became disturbed as overcrowding increased. Normal sexual behaviour of a male rat involves a passive phase and an active one, and it is always directed towards a receptive female. If a receptive female goes into a burrow the male will not follow her but waits at the entrance, intermittently putting his head into the burrow opening. Eventually when the receptive female re-appears the male pursues her and mounts her when she is over-taken. During copulation he holds her gently by the scruff of the neck with his teeth, taking care not to cut the skin. She arches her back as he makes the pelvic thrusting movements during intromission.

The passive phase is a time during which the male rat becomes convinced, from the clues he has picked up, that the rat he sees is a suitable partner: an adult rat, a female, and 'on heat' and so receptive to sexual advances. But the stress of overcrowding produced a breakdown in community life. The sexual behaviour of male rats no longer conformed to the well-established pattern. The passive phase, during which the male decided the other rat was ready for mating, disappeared completely. Males, instead of waiting at the entrance to burrows, would pursue the females down the burrow and into the nesting-boxes, thereby disturbing other female rats and their litters. This further aggravated the already disturbed pattern of the females when transporting the young to another nest.

The biting of the neck by the males during intercourse lost its gentleness; whereas before the skin of the female rat was not cut, now that an abnormal behaviour pattern was being followed severe nicks in the skin became apparent on their necks.

Another change observed in the behaviour of the male rats was their failure to identify rats ready for mating, that is, adult female rats 'on heat'. Females who showed no sign of being receptive were pursued and mounted. As overcrowding increased, sexual behaviour became even more disturbed. Male rats mounted both other males and young rats—male and female—who had just been weaned.

The normal aggressive behaviour of male rats underwent change too. When males came into conflict under normal conditions one rat, the loser, would eventually turn and flee and usually would be bitten on his posterior by the victor as he fled. This was the extent of normal aggressive behaviour. But as stress due to overcrowding increased, this quite moderate act of aggression was replaced by much more aggressive acts. Some males became tail-biters, clamping down on the tails of other rats and not loosening their grasp until the bitten rat had pulled its tail loose—frequently breaking or actually severing the tail in the process. Indiscriminate slashing attacks on other rats also became common. Both male and female victims received gashes ranging from 10 to 30 millimetres on all parts of the body.

The social stress also had its physiological effect, particularly on females. Pregnant females had very frequent miscarriages, failed to deliver babies and died at or before delivery. Fetuses died before delivery. Community life broke down almost entirely.

Need it happen to Man?

The parallel with Man living in overcrowded cities is obvious. These experiments help us to understand the dynamic social behaviour of groups living in a confined environment. But these responses occurred in a rat community whose geographical boundaries could not be extended, because the experimenters did not wish to do so. A similar situation need not be allowed to arise in human affairs. The south-east need not become a vast megametropolis. London need not grind to a halt. Overcrowding can be avoided if sufficient attention is paid to the problem. The rat experiment suggests some reasons why life in big cities is beginning to break down in areas where there is overcrowding.

People in towns are exposed to potentially stress-making situations through their contact with so many others at work, when travelling or when following outside leisure activities. Until fairly recently societies consisted of people who shared the same values. Everyone in the community had much the same cultural habits, speech, gestures and facial expressions. They also understood almost instinctively what sociologists called 'personal distance'—the distance people (especially the British) try to keep from others when in conversation, the distance we try to keep from others when we are in a crowd. Examples of 'personal distance' can be seen even in the London rush hours when travelling on commuter trains or on the Underground. Passengers try, as far as possible, to avoid physical contact with others in the crowd.

Rapid world transport now makes it possible for different nationalities and races to move to new territories and to mix with the people of other countries as never before. An almost instinctive dislike of outsiders, which has its roots in our animal ancestors, causes awkward situations to develop. Our attitudes towards outsiders show that stress is present.

In animals this is understandable—rats are stimulated to fight by the smell of a strange rat in the community—but in 'rational' Man, who has supposedly thrown off these behaviour patterns, such a reaction is prejudice.

It can be overcome by insight into our motives and an understanding of the factors which make up the situations. A long settling-in period is often needed before newcomers learn the local way of life. Even the movement of an individual or family from one region of the country to another can call out this prejudice. When people from the north of England first come into the London area they feel they are regarded as outsiders. But working against this prejudice and helping to break it down are the national television and radio programmes that tend to give people a common cultural base.

The rapidly changing social structure

The uncertainty that hangs over so much of modern life, its unpredictability, creates anxiety in many people. It is said that before the First World War the future seemed likely to be much the same as the present. Changes came slowly, perhaps stretching over several generations. Social standing, too, hardly changed in the lifetime of an individual. Depending on education and family circumstances, a young man would enter a profession and expect to be in it for the rest of his life.

Today the possibility of redundancy has to be faced by many in employment. They can no longer feel secure, for there is no guarantee, as there once seemed to be, that the daily routine will never alter. Today there are pressures at work tending to break down the small family unit of parents and children, just as job mobility once helped to destroy the 'extended family' of grandparents, uncles, aunts, parents and children. Manufacturers and their marketing specialists now split the small family unit into age groups, each with a different life style, that makes the 'generation gap' a reality rather than a journalist's cliché. The presence of these varying standards of value inside a family leads to conflict among its members and consequently to the stress response.

The movement towards equality of educational opportunity for both sexes has brought a change in family structures. The traditional family pattern of the father as the breadwinner and the mother as the housewife is becoming less common. This is not to say that the change is unwelcome; welcome or not it can be a cause of social stress.

Adapting to any major social change causes many people to experience a stress response. Nevertheless man is a resilient animal with the great advantage as a species of being adaptable. He has the intelligence and ability to foresee the future, although he is hampered by a reluctance to change his behaviour. In particular he has still to find a way to overcome hostility to outsiders—other people who have a colour, religion or ideology different from his own. He is faced with possible failure to cope with the effects of this powerful emotion, which is at work at a time when a worldwide common culture, based on the 'American way of life', is being created.

As yet research has failed to come up with an answer to the question: What are the limits of man's tolerance in certain situations? If we know the answer more accurately, then we can pinpoint those situations it is best to avoid because of the conflicts they generate.

Johan Galtung, Director of the International Peace Research Institute at Oslo, has suggested the development of a modern science of 'conflictology'. Other research institutes are following suit. For example there is the Centre for Conflict Resolution at the University of Michigan, where information in a number of fields is being drawn upon in an effort to make this subject, which will include international studies, sociology and behavioural psychology, a legitimate discipline for study.

Galtung emphasizes that schools should teach conflictology both as a practical exercise and as a subject for academic study. He wants conflict games to be devised, played and analysed by children so that ways of coping successfully with the stress of interpersonal relations can be found. He hopes that if children develop this ability they will carry it forward into adult life and perhaps help to avoid community conflict.

Groups of people with similar interests—for example prisoners and school children—that are not at present organized as trade unions are, should be encouraged to form participatory movements. Already in existence are such organizations as Encounter groups, consumer organizations (of which Nader's Raiders in the USA are an outstandingly successful example) and group therapy units. It is by membership of organizations like these that conflict and leadership problems are resolved. Galtung emphasizes that there must be an increase in making policy decisions, so that more people are involved in shaping the future. Such a movement would lessen the growing feeling among many of us that the wishes of the individual no longer matter. For it is this feeling—that in a complex society the democratic process is a sham—which produces despair, alienation and violent protest.

7 *Stress in Marriage*

When Richard was fourteen and at grammar school he had had what he thought was to be his last fight. The only instance of unladylike behaviour that his wife Helen could call to mind was when she was six and had pulled another girl's hair at a party. Yet in the third year of their marriage these two people were fighting each other with some ferocity.

During the course of consultations with the probation officer it became clear that Helen had deep-seated fears of being unloved, and constantly sought reassurance of her husband's affection for her. In the early part of the marriage he was able to give her this assurance by spending all his leisure time in her company, but promotion to another department brought with it the need to work late on certain occasions. The new job aroused his interest much more than the previous one; after staying late at the office he then brought some work home. In the morning he showed eagerness to get back to his desk, more so than ever before. In time, said Helen, 'my only contact with him was when we were at the same table or in the same bed'.

She began to regard his work as a rival for her husband's affection. Before, she had encouraged his ambitions; now she urged him to return to the poorer paid, run-of-the-mill job he had been doing before. When this plea failed the stress responses took their toll; she became ill, developing symptoms of headaches, feverishness, pains in various parts of the body. At first these items of her malaise were in evidence in the evening when Richard returned home. They caused him to spend some time preparing the meal and looking after his wife, so that he had less time to devote to the work he had brought home to do. But he tackled the situation by staying up later and rising early.

The wife's pattern of illness then changed. Her bouts of sickness occurred in the morning; often her husband was late in leaving for the office and on two occasions he stayed home until midday. The doctor assured Richard that there did not appear to be anything physically wrong with his wife. But the headaches and bouts of sickness continued, for the stress situation remained unchanged.

The doctor's comment made Richard believe that his wife was pretending to be ill, and he decided that the way to treat her malaise was to ignore it. From then on, although his wife might allege she had a bad headache when she woke or severe stomach pains, he got himself ready for work and left at the normal time.

One day when this happened Helen rushed from the bedroom as her husband was on his way to the front door. She caught hold of his wrists, dragged him back into the centre of the room and begged him not to leave her. To break free Richard had to struggle, and finally pushed his wife away. He stayed late deliberately at the office that night, and on arriving home appeared absorbed in making notes on a report he had brought with him. He refrained from going into the bedroom to see how his wife was feeling. In the middle of his work his wife came into the room and beat him about the shoulders with the metal pipe of a vacuum cleaner attachment, shouting: 'You're not going to ignore me!' An attempt at self-defence on the husband's part led to an all-in scrimmage.

Although immediately afterwards both of them were shamefaced about the incident and a temporary rapprochement was established, a fortnight later a similar scene occurred, and then another a few days later. By the time the couple asked for help from a social worker the fighting between them had become an almost daily occurrence.

Helen explained her use of force: 'My husband had no time for me. I needed him and I was determined to get his attention.

I didn't care if he hated me for it, I wasn't going to let him ignore me.' On another occasion when she took his clothes from the wardrobe and started to rip them up before his eyes she said: 'He *had* to notice me then.' Violence was a certain means of ensuring that she was at the centre of her husband's attention, at least during the time he was struggling with her. She wanted to be emotionally involved with him, and if she couldn't be loved she would settle for hate.

Talking over the situation both husband and wife agreed such behaviour was unacceptable. Yet they had lifted the ban on violence which they both in their more rational moments regarded as necessary. Richard's part in the scuffles was understandable. He had been brought up to regard striking a woman as something not done, but when attacked his impulse was to defend himself and to retaliate. Passive resistance is not an easy thing to practise on the spur of the moment when you are being hit with a metal pipe.

The early history of Helen revealed that for her the taboo on violence had been weakened by childhood experiences. She came from a lower middle-class family. She had always regarded her parents as happily married until one night, when she was about five years old, she had been awakened by sounds of shouting and blows coming from her parents' bedroom. She hammered on their door, but was unable to attract attention owing to the violent quarrelling inside. Her father never referred to the incident; her mother mentioned it once only, on the following day, when she said: 'It's nothing for you to worry about, dear. What goes on in bedrooms is secret.'

Children identify themselves with their parents. Helen may have had the subconscious fear that she would also be unable to control her temper. When the rift in her own marriage appeared she may have reconciled her own behaviour to herself by accepting her mother's statement that there are things inside marriage which are absolutely personal and cannot be judged by the standards of the outside world. It is difficult to put on one side the example set by one's parents.

Extremes of social stress

Stress situations inside a marriage sometimes reveal their existence when physical violence erupts. It did not do so in the Phillips's marriage referred to in the previous chapter possibly because Mr Phillips was entirely unassertive, accepting meekly his wife's strictures and decisions.

When violence does occur it is the most extreme form of social stress. It has to be admitted that we do not know how much violence there is in marriage. The research done is minimal, but probation officers and marriage guidance counsellors have a great deal of evidence of its existence. Among the working class it would seem to be on the decrease, as middle-class respectability is copied. As the institutional aspects of marriage are decreasing (less housework, less cooking, less washing done at home, children being cared for outside the home more than before), so the personal factors in marriage are increasing. And if a marriage partner is chosen not because of her value as housekeeper or cook, but as a companion, there is more danger of friction between the two and so the possibility of violence.

One factor which operates to conceal unhappiness in marriage is the 'bargain' element of the institution. No one likes to admit that he has bought a bad bargain in the shops; no one likes to admit that the marriage which started off with such high hopes is not turning out well. Even if one partner is solely to blame, the other may keep silent—at least for a time. Reticence about marriage often protects the aggressor from social disapproval.

Lifting the censorship

Peter, the chief clerk in a small importing business, a pleasant, inoffensive fellow, was well liked by the junior clerks and typist. Normally he was a sober fellow too, but at irregular intervals he became the worse for drink and then he frequently made physical attacks on his wife, Anna. When interviewed, she blamed drink for these outbursts, and emphasized that her husband was normally a very peaceable man who, if anything, was too easy going and allowed people to take advantage of him. Peter was apologetic about his behaviour, but, as he was able to blame alcohol for his lack of control, he was not deeply ashamed. He was, however, very upset about a single act of violence which occurred when he was sober. In the early hours of one morning he had punched his wife about the head and face when they were in bed together. 'I just can't account for that. Something came over me,' was his unhelpful explanation.

Alcohol by itself does not cause aggressiveness. It lessens self-control and so enables the censorship to be lifted on certain forms of behaviour. What was discovered as a result of looking into Peter's antecedent history was that his outbursts of violence corresponded approximately to the times when his employer was at the office. The employer, from all accounts a self-opinionated and ill-mannered man, travelled extensively, and invariably on his return criticized all that had gone on in the office during his absence and humiliated his chief clerk in front of the juniors. Peter's authority was strictly limited when his employer was present; what few gifts as an administrator Peter possessed were not allowed to function during these periods. This frustration, common among those who are in work which does not allow their aptitudes full play, had added to the resentment felt towards his employer. So there was a social stress situation built in to Peter's employment.

His subsequent behaviour illustrates the 'lightning conductor' aspect of some marriages. Hostile feelings aroused during the day are discharged in the home at night, particularly by those people with passive, rather ineffective, personalities. Instead of responding immediately to the stress situation by positive action, the 'fight' response is repressed for the time being and released later on a completely different target. Cruelty to children is often demonstrated by this type of parent. The violence brings relief to the aggressor because it is regarded unconsciously as positive behaviour. Unfortunately it is directed not against those persons who have caused the underlying resentment but towards someone who is quite innocent of creating hostility.

Among the middle class, violence has never been accepted even tacitly, so that marks of violence are not paraded defiantly. Both parties at first explain away the scratches and bruising. In time both realize that their stories are not likely to be believed, so they tell a close friend about their troubles, knowing that the story will slowly circulate and that in future no explanations of bruising and scratches need be given.

Social class

Andy and Cheryl came from different social groups. His parents had been small shopkeepers, her father was a doctor. There was strong parental disapproval of the marriage from the wife's side, and, unwisely handled by her father, this disapproval actually accelerated the marriage. They disagreed about many things, in particular about children. She wanted children; he did not. He had poor taste in clothes and she hoped to take over the buying of his wardrobe after marriage. He resented this. She was quickly brought to realize that her plans for changing her husband's outlook and general pattern of behaviour were not likely to be successful. In particular the disagreement about having a family led to arguments concerning contraception, to allegations, even when making love, that one was trying to outwit the other.

There was no flexibility in the approach Andy brought to his marriage. He came unwillingly to see the probation officer after his wife had asked for help, and showed he had little or no insight into his own behaviour. He could not accept that his own impulses or beliefs might be undesirable, judged objectively. He did not accept a further invitation to talk over the marital difficulties.

The violence came later. Cheryl became pregnant. Her husband declined to believe that he was responsible. He alleged that she had gone with another man in order to 'put one over' on him. He attacked his wife, tearing her clothes and bruising her, and turned her out of the house. It seems likely that he was punishing her not only for her supposed adultery, but for her superior social class, her attempts to make him conform to her standards, for her parents' disapproval of him as son-in-law. All these had been stress situations for him, which finally erupted into the 'fight' response when he was no longer able to control the force of his feelings. The veneer of restrained behaviour expected of 'civilized' people is always in danger of being shattered in a marriage, for here in a concentrated relationship social stress situations build up rapidly.

8 Children under Stress

An unusual reaction to a stress situation arising out of an unhappy marriage was shown by a sales manager. His wife applied to the magistrates for a separation order on the grounds that her husband, although living in the same house, had technically deserted her. When not at work or in bed he spent all his time with a much younger woman. But when a final break with his wife seemed imminent he became depressed and anxious. He went to see his doctor and as a result became an out-patient at the psychiatric clinic of one of the local hospitals.

It was this that weighed with the magistrates when the wife's application for a separation order came before them. They thought it indicated that the husband was still unwilling to make the final break with his wife in spite of his behaviour. So the case was adjourned for a probation officer to see the couple, in the hope of bringing about a reconciliation.

The husband would have been happy if the situation could have been left unchanged. He was having intercourse with the other woman two or three times a week, but when she pestered him to leave his wife and to build his life around her he began to experience feelings of acute anxiety. There appeared to be no rational basis for this anxiety; the man would earn a good living whether he lived with wife or mistress.

The findings of the psychiatrist revealed that the anxiety sprang from fears in the husband's childhood which the present situation had revived. He was a product of the slums, neglected by his parents, often hungry, always poorly clad. The girl had a similar background but had not risen in the social order as he had. Her manner of living was very much as it had always been. She liked Saturday night singing in the pub, spending all she earned, saving nothing.

The marriage had given the husband stability. With his wife, a careful manager, they had saved enough to buy the home they were living in, they owned their car and had over £1,000 in a building society account. He was fearful that in teaming up with the girl he would go back to the conditions of his childhood. He wanted to live with the girl but there was a conflicting impulse to stay with his wife. He feared that if he left his wife he would also leave the security he needed, and would be thrown back into insecurity that had made his childhood so unhappy. These fears conflicted with his desire to live with the girl. When he came to realize this through his talks with the psychiatrist, he gave up his friendship with her. At the root of the neurosis was the husband's unhappy childhood.

Mental conflict

Most of us have mental conflicts of some kind, and many of them are resolved quite easily. The impulse to have a really good meal is strong when we are trying to reduce weight. The conflict is resolved by one of the two impulses becoming dominant and influencing action. This of course does not amount to a neurosis. When the issue at stake is of great importance conflict becomes more serious, and often is incapable of an immediate solution. The two impulses continue to exist in the conscious or subconscious mind. Such a state of affairs is extremely stressful, often resulting in acute anxiety.

This is what happened to the sales manager. He developed a neurosis brought on by a conflict between two opposing impulses—to fall in with the wishes of the other woman and live with her, and to stay with his wife who represented the security he needed.

The children who suffer

It is arguable that stress situations in unhappy marriages cause as much illness, mental and physical, to the children of the marriage as they do to the parents.

The differing reactions of individuals to stress arising from similar circumstances is demonstrated in the behaviour of two brothers.

George, a boy of twelve, came into the juvenile court charged with a particularly vicious assault on one of his schoolmates in the playground. It was not an isolated outburst of violence on George's part; he had been displaying this behaviour pattern for two or three months. An investigation into his home environment made at the request of the magistrates showed that the outbursts of violence had developed only since his mother's departure from home. She and her husband were at loggerheads; she had disappeared without saying goodbye to either her husband or her children. The standard of home comfort for the children had fallen considerably, for their father was unable to look after them properly. His wife's desertion made him so apathetic that he did not ask neighbours for help, nor did he try to find someone willing to act as housekeeper.

George's reaction to the stress of the changed environment and the feeling that his mother no longer cared for him was one of rage. That of his younger brother, aged eight, was totally different. This boy, who was his mother's favourite, now developed nightmares which in their intensity woke the whole household. Finally the mother was traced and persuaded to return. But the younger child's nightmares continued, although their frequency lessened. The anti-social behaviour of George continued to create difficulties for more than a year.

No physical cause

Roger, a ten-year-old, was a regular witness of quarrels between his parents. During these quarrels his mother always threatened to leave home. Roger did not like his father, who showed little affection for the boy. Roger began to complain of abdominal pains; these were so severe that his mother kept him away from school whenever they came on. An examination by the school medical officer failed to reveal any organic cause. Later this failure to attend school brought him before the juvenile court.

Such a state of affairs is not at all uncommon. R. T. Stone and G. J. Barbero of Philadelphia, two American paediatricians, reported in 1966 on a survey in Philadelphia of children who complained of abdominal pains and disorders. Two-thirds of the children examined had previously been diagnosed as suffering from appendicitis, constipation or duodenal ulcer. The paediatricians were unable to find any anatomical or physiological cause for the abdominal pains, and they concluded that the symptoms were related to stress situations arising from some factor in the child's relationship with his environment.

The child from a broken home has often had to endure the denigration of one of his parents by the other. Their mutual antagonism and the abuse they heap on each other serve to diminish the child's image of them. And because a child is to a great extent a reflection of his parents, for he identifies with and imitates them, any denigration of them lessens his self-esteem. Children who think well of their parents are usually poised and self-confident. Those who do not are usually insecure and so more liable to develop feelings of anxiety.

These findings have been confirmed in many studies made of children referred for psychiatric treatment. In Edinburgh in 1961 one hundred primary school children receiving psychiatric treatment were compared with a similar number not emotionally disturbed. Only six children in the normal group came from broken homes, compared with twenty-eight of those receiving psychiatric treatment.

Death of a parent

The effect of bereavement, as a stress situation, depends on the make-up of the child. The resultant behaviour can be as diverse among children as it is among adults, varying from little or no response to mental illness or delinquency.

In a closely knit family, where the relationship between all its members is securely based on affection, the image of the dead parent can be sustained by the surviving parent, enabling the child to remember the dead parent with affection and pride, both of which contribute to the child's self-image. But research done by Dr Michael Rutter at the Child Psychiatric Department of the Maudsley Hospital in London showed that the death of a parent can create emotional disturbance in the child to such an extent that psychiatric treatment becomes necessary.

This is especially noticeable when the child is three or four years old, girls being more at risk than boys if the mother dies. The effect of the bereavement on the child is not immediately apparent; in nearly two-thirds of the children studied there was a time lag of five years or more before the symptoms of emotional disturbance showed themselves.

The existence of a five-year gap does not hold for adolescent boys. The research showed that they may display anti-social behaviour or depression within six months of the death of a parent, as did Harold in the case history that follows.

Harold was fourteen when his father died; within two months of the funeral he appeared in court on a charge of obtaining money by menaces from another boy.

Father had dominated the family; whenever the parents quarrelled Harold's mother invariably gave way. The boy came to despise her for this and to admire his father. After his father's death Harold asserted himself, attempting to dominate his mother as his father had done. His mother strongly resisted, and this resulted in many quarrels between her and her son. His aggression spilt over into other sectors of his life—school and youth club. He was threatened with loss of membership of the club, and his school behaviour brought him in conflict with members of the staff and finally into court.

Harold had not assessed his mother's character correctly. She was quite a determined woman, who had no intention of allowing her son to dominate her. What Harold did not realize was that his mother had given way to her husband so much because she feared that, if she opposed him, he would desert his family in order to live with a woman with whom he was associating. It is likely the antagonism between mother and son would not have arisen if the relationship between the two had been secure, but quarrelling between the parents had destroyed the normal relationship between mother and son.

Not *all* children who lose a parent by death become emotionally disturbed. There is no way of assessing accurately the proportion of bereaved children who do suffer in this way unless more research is undertaken.

It is not only the effect of the death on the unconscious mind that brings on the emotional disturbance. The alteration in family circumstances and the child's relationship with the remaining parent are also contributory factors.

The loss of a parent of the same sex hinders the development of a child's personality. Research has shown that a girl is more likely to be affected by the death of her mother and a boy by the death of his father. In their very early years children model themselves on the parent of the same sex. Studies done in America have revealed that of children who have lost a father, boys are more likely to have difficulty in their own sexual and marital adjustments when they become adult.

The chances are increased of a child becoming emotionally disturbed by the death of a parent if the child has been subjected to additional stresses, such as a bad relationship between the parents. This of course is in line with the Life-Change theory of Dr Holmes (*see* Chapter 1).

Going into hospital

Of the many stressful experiences to which children can be subjected, going into hospital is one of the most severe. For the child has to cope with a double anxiety. He is ill and so not able to follow a normal life. On top of this he is separated from the people to whom he is most attached—his parents. When the child has perhaps to undergo an operation involving an anaesthetic the stress is increased even more.

Children of all ages are affected, although the response to the stress of going into hospital and of being separated from parents differs according to the illness, age and personality of the child and the treatment received in hospital.

One of the most revealing studies of the effect on a child in hospital was carried out by a group of psychiatrists in Boston, U.S.A. Their work showed that, in spite of excellent medical care which indeed paid regard to emotional problems, children in the age group of four years and under remained disturbed while in hospital and presented many more behaviour problems than other children when they were discharged.

Surprisingly, the children who experience stressful situations before going into hospital, or who have an insecure relationship with parents, suffer the most. One would imagine these children would enjoy leaving a home where they are not particularly happy, yet the reverse is the case. It is the happy child who has the best chance of adjusting well to separation from parents. A child who is insecure at home cannot make a good adjustment away from home.

The way in which children in hospital can best be helped, so that emotional disturbance is not added to their other anxieties, is to allow parents to accompany a child on admission and to be involved in the hospital care provided.

The need for this involvement of the parent (and particularly the mother) with the hospital has been underlined by many investigations made by paediatricians and psychiatrists. It has been given official blessing by the Platt Report on the Welfare of Children in Hospital, published in 1959. The recommendations are now the official policy of the Department of Health, but many provincial hospitals still refuse to carry out the report's recommendations. By their refusal to accept the findings both of medical research and the Royal Commission they greatly add to the anxieties of children and parents.

An organization which works for the acceptance by hospitals of the Commission's recommendations is the National Association for the Welfare of Children in Hospital, Exton House, 7 Exton Street, London SE1 8VE. As the association points out, there should be no general rule restricting the visiting of child patients immediately prior to or after any operation. As far as both unrestricted visiting and mothers' accommodation are concerned, hospitals frequently say that where both these facilities are available they are under-used. This is probably true. It simply indicates, first, that not enough has been done to make it more widely known that children in hospital need their parents, and secondly, the need to provide local supporting services, such as home helps and other types of community worker, to make it easier for parents to visit and to live in where necessary.

All parents should be allowed to visit their children without restriction when they are in hospital, and all mothers should be offered the opportunity to remain overnight with very young children. These facilities should be made available in all hospitals admitting children, with the staff actively encouraging parents to make use of them. Officials of the Department of Health have been urging hospitals for the past fourteen years to put this policy into practice.

In the United States there is an Association for Child Care in Hospital, but this is a professional association of doctors, nurses, recreational staff, hospital teachers and social workers. It does not include parents. The lack of a unified hospital service in America means that standards vary enormously. There are hospitals that encourage parents to stay with their children (and one even makes a reduction in cost for the work the mother does in looking after her child), but there are many more that do not. Lacking a document akin to the Platt Report those hospitals practising progressive policies of parent involvement are likely to remain in the minority for a long time.

The burns unit

Guilt feelings and distress are common in families where one of the children has had an accident resulting in burns. Such accidents frequently happen in large families living in overcrowded conditions. Mothers feel guilty, blaming themselves for negligence;

this guilt may be increased if the hospital staff (who are often of a higher social/economic class than the parents) fail to understand both the guilt feelings of the parents and the day-to-day problems facing the family.

Research has been conducted at the Burns Unit of a Birmingham hospital where no special regard was being paid either to the emotional effects of the accident on parents and child or to the effect of the hospital treatment on the child. This latter may be particularly distressful, for it includes surgical treatment for skin grafting, pain when dressings are changed and the possibility of scarring. Visiting time at this hospital was strictly limited. Parents of babies and toddlers were allowed to see their children only from outside the glass-walled wards. No closer contact was permitted.

Of 198 children discharged from this Burns Unit, 80 per cent were found to be emotionally disturbed one year after discharge, compared with 7 per cent of unburnt brothers and sisters of the ex-patients. Symptoms of emotional disturbance included disorders of sleeping and eating, bed-wetting, aggressiveness and anxiety. Over half the mothers of these children were emotionally upset and nervy; one in six was being treated for what is commonly called a nervous breakdown.

As a result of the research, changes in hospital practice were introduced. Unrestricted visiting for all children was permitted. A psychiatric social worker was appointed to meet the parents of children in the unit and to help them with their emotional problems arising from the accident.

These meetings continued even when the child left hospital. It was found that giving help to parents and children with their emotional problems, together with the improved visiting facilities in the hospital, greatly reduced the number of disturbed children. Whereas the figure stood at 80 per cent before the changes were introduced, it fell to 20 per cent after the scheme had been working for a year.

The stress situation of being separated from mother can of course result when it is the mother who goes into hospital, or for some other reason has to be parted from her child. Then the progress made in socially acceptable behaviour (toilet training, for example) can be lost, and moodiness and temper tantrums can become common in children who never displayed them before.

And just as the disastrous effect on a young child of having to go into hospital can be avoided by the hospital authorities paying attention to the emotional needs of their young patients, so can similar upsets be avoided when it is the mother who goes away to have another baby, an operation or a period of convalescence. This was demonstrated in a research project conducted in 1972 by James and Joyce Robertson of the Tavistock Institute of Human Relations. The Robertsons acted as foster parents to a number of children between the ages of seventeen months and two years who were shortly to be separated from their parents, for one reason or another. All the children had had a happy home life, were developing normally and had not been separated from their mothers before.

The Robertsons prepared themselves well beforehand foı the duties of foster parents. During the four to six weeks preceding the separation of child and mother, they visited the homes, learned the ways the parents handled the child, made notes of sleeping patterns and food likes and dislikes, and memorized favourite nursery rhymes and the special words which child and parents used for various objects. The children also visited the Robertsons in their home so that they would not be unfamiliar with their new surroundings when the time came for fostering.

The experiment proved a success. It showed that with the majority of young children a carefully planned separation from mother can occur without the aftermath of emotional disturbance. But the foster parent must take the trouble to learn something of the child's way of life in order to reduce the demands made on the child by the new situation.

In the course of their report the Robertsons cite the behaviour of a child of seventeen months who went into a residential nursery for a few days while the mother was in hospital. Members of the staff of the nursery were not given responsibility for individual children and so no personal relationships could be formed. This child showed all the symptoms of disturbance that are displayed by children who have to stay in hospitals where little or no attention is paid to their emotional needs. He screamed when his mother eventually came for him, and for many weeks afterwards demonstrated aggression, temper tantrums and a refusal to eat that were until then foreign to his nature. A gulf between child and parents had been created by the separation.

In contrast, the close relationship that can grow up between nurses and a child patient can disturb the parent-child relationship if parents are not continuously involved with medical staff in caring for their child in hospital. Should the parent-child relationship be defective in any way the gulf between child and home can widen.

Christopher was born with a harelip. He was the first child and, as occasionally happens in marriages, the father was slightly jealous of the attention lavished on the boy by the mother, attention which was the greater because of the boy's defect. During the first eight years of his life Christopher underwent a number of operations, each necessitating a long period in hospital. There the nurses made a fuss of him; in time he came to enjoy being in the ward more than being at home, where his father's scarcely concealed jealousy and, with the arrival of other children, the loss of his mother's total attention made him feel something of an outsider. At the hospital visiting by relatives was strictly limited, so that his contacts with his family were slight. His mother was his principal visitor, his father rarely came.

When surgery was completed (and the harelip hardly noticeable) Chris found it hard to settle into the normal life of home and school. Extremely pleasant in manner, he was also quite detached in his attitude towards his family. Unemotional and apparently unthinking of the hurt he gave, he stole money from home whenever the chance presented itself. When the thefts were discovered he denied all knowledge of them. When his guilt was proved he appeared unmoved, unrepentant. He appeared in the juvenile court when, almost as a last resort, the parents asked the magistrates for help on the grounds that he was getting beyond their control. It was not until he left school and started work that some degree of stability was achieved.

9 Stress in Employment

Lionel was one of hundreds of thousands of youngsters who are forced into unsuitable employment and who for the most part go through life never realizing their true capabilities, often never voicing their secret ambitions. Anyone not given the opportunity to develop what talent he possesses is condemned to years of continuous response to stress, stress that arises from spending eight hours a day doing something that is not enjoyed. How much does such a situation, multiplied a million times, contribute to industrial strife, irritability, depression, family quarrels, marital tension and the reduced resistance that leads to ill health?

Lionel's father was a miner. Two elder brothers were also down the pit, and the neighbourhood was peopled by folk whose lives were centred on the colliery. Family tradition was strong. It is not surprising that when Lionel was seen during his last few months at school by the careers officer he had no job ideas. Brain-washing by the family led him to mutter 'Going down the pit.' That statement made the job of the careers officer so much easier; he probed no further.

From the outset Lionel disliked the colliery, the NCB Training Scheme and everything about pit life. He was a 'loner' who did not get on well with other trainees. All this quickly showed in his work record. Illness and absenteeism made him an unsatisfactory employee, finally resulting in his dismissal. Then followed one job after another, all dead-end occupations which he obtained either through his own efforts or through the youth employment officer. Never once was it suggested that he should take an aptitude test to ascertain the type of employment for which he was best suited.

This state of affairs radically changed for Lionel when he broke the law. He came into court for an unusual offence of stealing a dog. The animal belonged to a scrap merchant in the neighbourhood. Lionel had seen it tied up when taking rag to the scrap yard. He told me afterwards—but was too inarticulate to say it in court or to the police—that what had disturbed him was that the dog was always tethered, never allowed to leave the yard, never taken for a run, in fact a prisoner for life.

The lad climbed over the fence into the yard one Saturday night, when the scrap dealer and his family were out, and scrambled back again with the dog under his arm, the animal barking furiously all the time. Disaster followed. The dog was uncontrollable. Never having been out of the yard it went berserk, possibly with joy, straining on the rope and finally breaking away from its rescuer. It ran madly through the streets, not stopping until it was knocked down and killed by a car.

Lionel arrived on the scene to find the car driver explaining to a police officer what had occurred. If the lad had kept in the background and held his tongue he would never have appeared in court, but his concern for the dog led him to admit his part in the affair.

Latent talent

In the course of his period on probation more became known of Lionel's secret ambition. His sole interest appeared to be with animals. He was a keen pigeon fancier and kept rabbits, hamsters and a grass snake. Through the interest of a local veterinary surgeon, who was prepared to offer him a job, he became a veterinary assistant and was able to put his love of animals to good use.

Lionel was one who 'got away'. If he had not broken the law he might still be leading a life of spirit-killing frustration like millions more of those in his social class.

It has been estimated that eight million people in Britain are in wrong jobs. Much of the blame lies with the failure of the community to give vocational guidance the priority it deserves, a state of affairs that has produced a Schools Career Service of poor quality and the appointment in some schools of career masters and mistresses who are not given proper facilities to do the job well. And as a country we are still living with a tradition that has never considered rank and file workers to be anything more than an expendable labour force.

The failure of the combined efforts of the Youth Employment Service and careers teachers is reflected in figures showing the number of times less well-qualified boys and girls from the lower income groups have changed their jobs. Those who left school the earliest, at fifteen, made the most changes: 76.5 per cent had between one and five jobs; 17.6 per cent between six and ten jobs; 3.9 per cent between eleven and fifteen jobs. Only 2 per cent of the fifteen-year-olds kept the same jobs. Of those who left school at sixteen, 35.9 per cent changed their jobs between one and five times; 50 per cent between six and ten times, and 10.4 per cent between eleven and fifteen times; 3.7 per cent of the sixteen-year-olds kept the same job.

Discrimination against girls

Girls are at a greater disadvantage than boys in finding work suited to their talents. Renee Short, MP, chairman of the Parliamentary Expenditure Committee's sub-committee investigating the employment services, had this to say about the totally inadequate opportunities available for girls in employment: 'Careers teachers should be as well trained as careers officers in the Youth Employment Service, especially as their responsibilities towards girls and their jobs are so pressing. How badly their opportunities compare with boys'!

'Brain-washed into their conventional sex role from picture-book stage, few break through the limited horizons offered to them. They are offered clerical or secretarial work, shop work, or unskilled work in industry if they leave school early. The girls miss out on apprenticeships and day release. Forty-two per cent of boys but only 7 per cent of girls enter apprenticeships, and three-quarters of those are in hairdressing. Employers make more use of the provision of day release education for their young male employees than for their young female workers; 40 per cent of boys aged fifteen to seventeen get day release but only 10 per cent of girls. For many young people, especially the disadvantaged, day release is their only means of continuing their education after they leave school, yet of the whole age group only 12 per cent get any. The case for compulsory day release is irresistible.

'Discrimination continues during the whole of the working life of the girls who leave school early and who receive little or no training. Few of them manage to get selected for government training centres. In 1971 only sixteen women reached this exalted state. The Industrial Training Boards do little for women, orientated as they are towards the training of managers, and there are few women managers in industry.

'Even when women are accepted for industrial rehabilitation courses they receive a lower training allowance than men, £10.75 for the woman, £11.75 for the man—both low enough indeed.'

At all examination levels from the CSE upwards there are fewer subject entries for girls; only 28 per cent of university students are female, only one out of twenty managers is a woman, and only a fraction of 1 per cent of scientists, technologists or draughtsmen are women.

Until 1960 a Ministry of Education ruling was in operation for the construction of schools. This stated that a lower standard of accommodation for science should be provided for girls' and mixed schools than for boys' schools. All schools built before 1960 carry this sex prejudice in their design.

To have an aptitude in a certain direction—a basic innate capacity—and not to be allowed to develop it is certain to generate frustration. For if aptitudes are not recognized, ability can never be shown and so achievement is out of the question.

The 'housewife syndrome'

By discrimination of this sort society creates stress situations for women, resulting in a stunting of personality growth. Yet in spite of this married women persist in seeking paid employment. In so doing they may avoid catching what some medical men call the 'housewife syndrome'—aches and pains, apathy, irritability and tiredness, often associated with an inability to sleep. Currently doctors in Holland are investigating this syndrome, which is brought on partly by frustration because the woman's job as housewife is not satisfying to her, and partly by doubts she entertains about the value of her role, for she is not paid for doing it and it is not regarded as a profession in its own right.

Some women, especially those who have been trained for a professional job, suffer in another way when they have to give up work to have a baby.

Such a woman was Mrs Shelley, living on the outskirts of a large industrial city. She called her condition 'suburban stagnation'. Her doctor labelled it one-baby neurosis, implying that when the second one came along she would be too busy to feel discontented with her lot. Hers was not a physical manifestation as it is in the 'housewife syndrome', but boredom.

She had stayed on after her marriage at the laboratory where she was employed, working almost up to the time of the baby's birth. She and her husband had bought a new house on mortgage on one of the private building estates on the city's perimeter. Although they were now quite a long way from old friends and relatives they still had the stimulus of contact with fellow workers, the tea-break discussions, the many opportunities to talk 'shop', which is the most absorbing topic for an intelligent person doing the right job.

But for Mrs Shelley all this was cut off overnight when she resigned to become a mother. At first the excitement of having the baby concealed her loss. 'It was marvellous to have baby and to wash the nappies,' she told me, 'but when I had got into the routine I suddenly began to feel discontented—and guilty. I used to ask myself, "Why do I feel so discontented? I've got a nice home and a nice child and nice neighbours." One day I went back to the laboratory to see them all. I could have sat down at the bench and gone on from where I left off. When I came away I knew what was missing. It was all the talk that went on about the job.'

'After a year away from the laboratory all I could talk about was baby,' says Mrs Shelley. 'How I fed him, what he weighed. I was not lonely in the physical sense; there are plenty of people to talk to at the shops and the clinic, but it was always the same conversation. Our babies—what they weighed, how we fed them. One night my husband and I went out to dinner with some people from the lab. It was a special occasion of some kind. I found I hadn't got any conversation at all. When I'd said my piece about baby that was it.'

The answer was to get back to work again, but with family responsibilities this could not be done immediately. So she had to look around for an activity that would keep her mentally alert and avert in part the stress situation caused by boredom.

'Reading was not the answer,' she said. 'Although we have the posh Sunday papers and all that, and I'm in the library, it's actual conversation on a fairly high level that's needed. To get your brain working you need to discuss with people of your own kind—and if possible with someone more intelligent—a topic of importance. Casual, undirected talk is not enough.'

Alleviating boredom

By making known her views Mrs Shelley came to hear of the Housewives' Register. With four other young mothers she formed a group of the register in her neighbourhood. As a result of this action she partly solved her problem. The idea of the Housewives' Register was put forward by Mrs Maureen Nichol of Cheshire in a letter to the *Guardian* in 1960, after she had read an article about the mental stagnation of some suburban housewives. Further publicity in the *Observer* and *Sunday Times* resulted in a great many young mothers writing to Mrs Nichol in the hope that she would take the initial steps to get the register established. She did so by appointing regional organizers to answer letter-writers from the locality and to make introductions. Today there are several hundreds of organizers and many thousands of members.

The only qualification for membership, according to the official pamphlet, is the possession of a lively and inquiring mind interested in the exchange of ideas. The majority on the register have had some sort of professional training for a career, a good many are married to professional men, all enjoyed bringing up a family but did not want household chores to become all-absorbing. Another point which emerges is the mobility of this social class. One of the young mothers in Mrs Shelley's group, the wife of a technical college lecturer, has moved house three times since her marriage as a result of her husband's improving his status. Being 'on the register' means that the member can obtain the names and addresses of other members in the district to which she is moving, thus cutting short the time usually taken in making friends of similar outlook and education.

Because of the common desire of members to think about something more than running a household, most of the groups do have a monthly get-together with a local speaker. Meetings are held at the homes of members in turn, the hostess looking after all the babies while the discussion goes on in another room. A group on an estate a few miles away from Mrs Shelley had discussions during the past winter months on retail price maintenance, delinquency, insecticides, the modern theatre and the care of the old. Sometimes the speaker is a visitor; often members do research and present their findings as a basis for discussion.

Mrs Shelley was fortunate in that she had shown an aptitude for laboratory work and had been trained to the point where her ability gave her some status and a good salary. But many women who are bored by domestic chores find that when seeking employment they can only find work which is also frustrating. As a leader in the *Guardian* put it recently: 'How often, for example, has one heard the subject of working wives discussed only in the context of "interesting and rewarding career", "doing the work her education fitted her for," and so on. It is forgotten that for many, perhaps a majority of wives, the return to work after having a family may be to a dull, repetitive, and perhaps arduous job in a factory.'

This is only one of the stress situations to be faced by mothers who do go out to work, and it is made more acute by the lack of nursery schools and play groups.

Guilt feelings

It will be recalled that in giving the case history of Mrs Phillips, who attempted suicide, reference was made to her work as an office cleaner. Just how much this job increased the strain on her and so helped to bring about her deterioration cannot be assessed. The vast majority of women work either inside the home or outside or both. One woman in three earns money at an outside job either full time or part time. We know that the stress situations encountered when earning a living in a male-orientated society are considerable. The mother who goes out to work often has a feeling of guilt, in spite of the fact that research has shown that she is often a better mother as a result of working. Women who stay at home tend to have a restricted outlook and are often lonely.

But if success in being a working mother means having a well-paid job and a happy family plus freedom from strain, this ideal woman is almost non-existent. The pattern of the working mother has not yet established itself in society. The old traditions and beliefs about 'a woman's place' still linger on. It will certainly take another decade for working mothers to get free of this legacy of guilt.

In the Government Statistical Surveys' publication, *Social Trends*, the number of working mothers was given as 2,097,000 for the year 1966. More than 50 per cent of these had more than one child, and 2,074,000 school-age children between five and fifteen had working mothers. This is about a quarter of the total school population; 515,000 children below the age of four also had mothers who went to work. The number of working mothers has increased since 1966; today one mother in three works part or full time. This description 'working mother' for a mother who goes out to work is a bad one, for the mother who stays at home works too—for nothing. And she walks 8½ miles a day in the process of shopping, cooking, cleaning and looking after the children, say time and motion experts. Nevertheless we shall have to stick by the inaccurate description.

The difficulty which many a working mother faces, of having to leave her children for another woman to look after, is the general cause of the stress situation. She can rarely be sure she can give undivided attention to her work. There is always a possibility of a telephone call from the substitute mother asking for a decision or posing a problem. The stress differs according to the social class of the mother. What counts is not so much what she earns as the job she does and the attitude of the community in which she lives.

Some 84 per cent of all working mothers claim that the children actually benefit by the arrangement, both materially and intellectually. In the upper and middle classes the main difficulty is the guilt feeling. Discussions with women in professional and managerial jobs show that these guilt feelings are almost universal, part of the penalty to be paid for following one's bent and at the same time earning money to pay for someone else to take care of the children. This guilt persists, setting up the stress response in the mind, however kind and efficient the mother-substitute may be. The guilt is quite irrational. Research done by Dr Simon Yudkin and Anthea Holme, contained in their book *Working Mothers and their Children*, shows that children actually benefit by having a mother at work but, as has been said, although women are convinced that their going out to work benefits the children, this knowledge does little to remove their guilt feelings, so heavily impregnated are they with the traditional beliefs about 'mother's place is the home'.

Middle-class wives

The working mother from the middle class spends most of her income on raising the standard of education and feeding and clothing of her children. Although this fact is obvious both to her and her husband, she still feels guilty about going out to work. Why should this be so? In some cases the guilt is present because there is a sense of inadequacy about being a mother. The woman feels she is more efficient in her career than in being a natural mother. She has been conditioned by the traditions of society to believe there is something wrong with a woman who rejects the responsibilities of motherhood and, if there are no children, the elementary function of child-bearing.

She puts in a great amount of effort to compensate for her supposed lack of maternal love. She worries over her children's health and education, over substitute mothers, over the influence of au pair girls and cleaning women. At the same time she is motivated to succeed in her profession, in the course of which she often has to compete with childless women and with male workers who can concentrate solely on a career, a state of mind she cannot achieve.

This sense of guilt is frequently accentuated by the attitudes of non-working wives in the community in which she lives. In prosperous suburban areas there are always households where wives do not go out to work, but who nevertheless have au pair girls and home helps to lighten the burden of domestic chores. Defending their way of life, these stay-at-home women unite to form cliques. The working mother then becomes the outsider. The clique feels that the mother who works for money is implying by her example that her neighbours are incapable of making any independent mark on life, and that they are parasitic types solely dependent on their husbands.

Group disapproval takes a number of forms. There can be a lack of warmth when the stay-at-homes meet the working mother, and the latter becomes accustomed to such barbed remarks as 'Of course I would love to lead an exciting life like yours but I cannot bear to leave the children.' This bitching is lessened only if the profession chosen by the working mother carries a high social status. If she is a doctor or even a teacher she is regarded as doing a job which serves the community. In fact very few working mothers—perhaps one in twenty—follow a professional career. A 1968 government survey shows that seven out of ten working mothers go to work simply to earn money, and at the time of the survey most earned less than five shillings (25p) an hour. They relied on grandmothers, mothers-in-law and occasionally husbands to care for the children. This figure of course has increased since the survey was made.

Working-class attitudes

In working-class communities there is far less guilt and far less bitching. The working-class community has been forced to accept, because of economic pressures, that the mother has to go to work. But the situation may still contain elements of stress. The lower-paid working-class mother is unable to afford an au pair girl and her evenings are spent in catching up with the washing, ironing, house cleaning and cooking. For these women the day's work is split into two shifts—one at the place of employment and one at home, the interval between the two being taken up with putting the children to bed. These mothers suffer a reaction to stress because they have a job which makes no allowance for school holidays or for the children to have those bouts of sickness from which they all occasionally suffer. There is the agony of indecision when the children are at home ill, or when the weather is bad, or when the alarm clock fails. Should the mother stay at home and lose money, bearing in mind that too much absence may jeopardize her job, or depute her home duties to go to work? Often neighbours are asked to care for the children, or an older child is kept from school to look after the younger one.

Many mothers on all social levels make complex arrangements to enable them to work. Working mother and journalist Patricia Keiran, in her investigation on this subject, reporting in her book *How Working Mothers Manage*, described how to be a successful working mother. Finding a reserve of helpers in illness or accident, planning meals without being able to go to the shops at will, looking for a holiday help who will keep the children from trouble and make up for mother's absence—these are but some of the multitude of organizational chores that are the lot of working mothers at all levels.

Where resentment exists in the marriage the working mother faces more tension than one from the middle class. Mrs Keiran warned readers who were considering going out to work of this possibility. The family soon gets used to the higher standard of living which the mother's income helps to provide. If for some reason she stops working, or goes to work part time only, it is difficult to adjust to a lower income, and this can cause some family resentment.

Should her income be used to pay school fees, it may be impossible at a certain stage to transfer the children from the fee-paying school to State schools, quite apart from the upset this would cause the children themselves. If the mother's income helps with a mortgage, it may be impossible for her husband to keep up the mortgage payments solely out of earnings.

The husband's role

Some husbands and fathers resent not being able to be the sole supporter of the family. These men feel that they are losing their masculinity and that they are diminished in the eyes of their children, even though the children have no such thoughts.

Making a success of going to work depends for a wife on the approval and help she gets from her husband. Ideally she needs a partner who does not depend on her money for the family's living standard. She needs a man who realizes that during the week she may be too tired to make love. She needs a husband who will get up to attend to a child with toothache or who needs a drink, she needs a husband who will put the children to bed when she is working overtime, and one who is proud to have a wife with interests outside the home. If the husband should contribute less to household expenses when the wife starts working, she may in turn resent her money being spent on tobacco and drink by her husband.

The key to the situation being handled successfully is the attitude of the husband. How can tensions be lessened? The main need is for the husband to help his wife to work without her having to worry about the children, and this can only be done by providing reliable and adequate care for the children—in other words having a reliable mother substitute. On the other hand, says Patricia Keiran, if the husband really and truly does not want his wife to work, she would be far better to dismiss the idea from her mind.

In 1968 the child care needs of Britain's working women required 536,000 nursery places, 318,000 nursery school places and 1,105,500 places for after-school care. The total is now much greater, and the provision pitifully small. Although the economy and the rapidly rising cost of living are forcing more and more mothers out to work, assistance by the State is totally inadequate to help the working mother play her part.

Little is known of proper child care facilities today. Only about 6 per cent of all children up to two years old are in day nurseries, and two-thirds of the State nurseries are in London and the north-west. Fewer than 100,000 of the 2,700,000 children who are eligible in fact benefit from nursery schools. Still less is known of the flourishing child-minding industry, many establishments being conducted without a licence and therefore never inspected. The Advisory Centre for Education's current research project into this unexplored area is likely to show how calamitous—certainly for the children concerned—is this situation. Some industrial concerns provide play groups and crèches for the children of their women employees, but not enough have these facilities. In some areas organizations, such as banks, employ women on the basis of two for the price of one. Both work part time taking turn about with child-minding and the job at the bank.

Social surveys indicate that fathers are becoming more willing to help with house and children, and among educationalists there are signs of a unisex approach to career training which will replace the traditional idea that men are suitable only for certain types of employment and women for other types.

Irritating the public

The colossal failure to ascertain an individual's potential in employment and to ensure that the worker is placed in a job which holds his or her interest is one reason that 35 per cent of the four hundred million working days lost annually is due not to organic but to psychological and functional illness which can arise from the body's response to stress.

Being unsuited to your job not only makes you irritable and ill but also deeply affects the people with whom you come into contact. Much of the bad feeling that exists between civil servants who have to 'meet the public'—customs and excise officers, counter clerks at employment exchanges and social security offices—is due to the civil service custom of drafting these officials into such jobs without bothering to find out if they are the type who are happy dealing with people. One would have thought that the Civil Service with all the expertise it can command would have taken the trouble to give aptitude and personality tests to the staff to ensure that those *drafted* to meet the public are keenly interested in people and their problems, and above all wish to do the job. The majority of civil servants on the opposite side of the counter from the general public do not wish to be there at all. Far fewer complaints would be received—and less stress generated—if only those with the aptitude and personality to handle people were drafted to those posts.

The industrial process

Technological progress and its application to industry have over the years led to the breakdown of the traditional craft processes. Much factory work is today a succession of repetitive tasks from which the worker gains little or no satisfaction.

He is no longer of any account, merely a very small cog in the machine. The feeling of participation and responsibility which some of the old craftsmen possessed has been lost. Much of to-day's factory work is drudgery, consequently there is a great amount of absenteeism and changeover of jobs, plus demands for higher wages to compensate for the tedium of the work.

The factory worker lacks the education to make himself materially successful in an age in which status is largely determined by wealth. Trapped in the system, it is not surprising that some young workers turn to violence and crime as an outlet in order to establish personality, while the older worker lives only for the out-of-work hours.

How little concern is shown for these factory floor workers is seen, for example, by the operation of the shift system. This disrupts family life, keeps husbands and fathers from their wives and children at the time when they should be getting together for the enjoyment of leisure. Yet it is insisted upon by employers to keep expensive machinery working round the clock in spite of the fact that it has a harmful effect on workers' health. The industrial process is considered of more importance than the well-being of the individual worker and his family. As in most of the environmental stress situations, other interests are allowed to take precedence over the well-being of the individual. It is no surprise that factory floor workers, who get less job satisfaction than, say, draughtsmen or designers or management, also have the biggest absenteeism rate.

Prince Philip, president of the Institute of Work Study Practitioners, put the situation succinctly when he gave his presidential address to the institute in 1972. He emphasized that industrialists should not ignore the human element when seeking ways of improving business methods. One aspect of work study derived from a traditional attitude towards industrial work-efficiency, productivity for economic gain and the best use of human and material resources.

It was just as important, he said, to solve the problems of human relationship to work.

'I believe the most important step towards a better attitude to the problem is to get out of the habit of referring to people as a resource. We must get away from the concept of education and training as a process of preparing and turning out people qualified for industry or commerce.

'I wonder whether it is really possible to go on squeezing higher and higher standards of efficiency and productivity out of people without improving the quality of the work they are invited to perform. A great many more jobs could be made much more satisfying. Somehow or other this critical element of satisfaction must enter the work study calculations at some point.'

There is no lack of knowledge that hinders us from placing workers in jobs suited to their aptitudes, ability and personality. In some large firms, industrial psychologists already operate to prevent square pegs from being driven into round holes. The procedure ensures that the employees are used to their own and the firm's best advantage, for working in the wrong job only produces stress situations and the probability of physical and mental ill health.

But, such is the attitude of management towards the working class, only employees at managerial and executive level are given the advantage of skilled job placement by industrial psychologists. The worker on the factory floor is ignored. This is just one reason why industrial unrest, strikes and absenteeism are rife among the lower income groups and almost entirely absent from the managerial and executive classes.

10 Stress Used as a Weapon

Some stress situations are an everyday occurrence; others happen perhaps only once in a lifetime. Of the former, the body's continued response has a long-term debilitating effect. The noise from the steel works gradually deafened the steel worker whose marriage was threatened by his disability. At any time during his years in the steel works he could have delayed or stopped the deterioration had he been aware of what was happening.

In some situations there is no such escape. Man deliberately constructs stress situations in order to injure his fellow men. War is the obvious example. Those involved in combat continue to react and show the stress response long after the cause has been removed. Examples are to be found in the records of the two world wars. Soldiers exposed to shelling and bombs have remained paralysed with fear even after removal to hospital in safe areas far away from the battle zone. These are extreme examples, but they do demonstrate what can happen if stress is continuous. Life is a continual series of adjustments, of responding to stress situations and adapting to them. Our physical and mental make-up decides how long we can stand out against continual stress. Everyone has a breaking point. Even the most resolute can be reduced after a sufficiently long period of hardship, fatigue, discouragement and disappointment to a state where self-control gives out and irrational impulse takes over.

R. C. Sherriff's play *Journey's End* is based on his own experience in World War I and the characters are drawn from life. Captain Stanhope, the company commander, sets a higher standard for himself than he does for others. After three years in the front line he could have taken promotion and a job at the rear; his self-imposed high standard of conduct does not permit this. He stays on, deteriorating gradually, his nerves battered by the immense man-made pressures of the external environment. A fellow officer, Hibbert, cracks up after only a few months in the line, demonstrating how variable is the individual response to stress. He lacks the power to adapt to the stress situations of trench warfare and his breaking point is quickly reached.

No one is surprised that people engaged in war suffer the effects of environmental stress. All the outward signs that one associates with stress are plain to see—noise, danger to life and limb, sudden catastrophes, uncongenial living conditions and periods of intense action followed by long periods of boredom when nothing significant happens.

The stress response to combat

Much research has been done on combat casualties of World War II. One of the most revealing investigations was carried out by the American psychiatrist Roy Swank, who studied some five thousand combat casualties of the Normandy campaign.

The first reaction of these men to combat was fear, but in time most of them controlled their fears and gained confidence as they became more proficient in live combat. Nevertheless, after this confidence had been achieved through expertise, there was a subsequent period in which combat exhaustion displayed itself.

It varied in severity according to individual experience. As a result of this and other investigations—including those made by Sir William Sargant, who dealt with several thousands of both civilian and service patients in the neurosis units of British Emergency Medical Service hospitals—it is now accepted that practically all combat soldiers eventually suffer from a neurotic reaction if they are subjected day after day and for long periods to the strain of battle.

The findings of Swank and Sargant prove that breakdown in battle cannot be resisted by either courage or strength of will;

in fact the opposite appears to be true. The man who runs away because he is fearful is not likely to suffer a breakdown. The continual exercise of will-power, screwing up one's courage—as those do who remain in the line of battle for too long—exhausts the brain and hastens final collapse in certain circumstances, says Sargant.

In his book, *Battle for the Mind*, Sargant points out that under normal conditions the nervous system is in a state of equilibrium between extreme excitement and an almost complete absence of movement. Under excessive stimulation, such as continuous combat, the body passes rapidly from the first stage to the second. The state of equilibrium, the normal poise which we show in everyday life, vanishes completely. For the time being the brain is incapable of functioning normally. Sargant quotes several examples from medical literature of front-line soldiers (who had hitherto appeared normal) becoming greatly excited and running at random towards the enemy or dashing suicidally into machine-gun fire. One soldier in an excitatory state advanced twice under enemy fire to rescue a friend whose leg was blown off. On arrival at the friend's side a period of inhibition took over, and on both occasions he failed to give first-aid to his friend. When this period passed, he was again overcome by acute excitement and kept banging his head against a tree and rushing wildly around shouting for an ambulance. On the arrival of an ambulance he forcibly strapped himself into it.

Another soldier, after his friend's death, attempted to tackle an enemy tank single-handed in a fit of sudden and intense excitement. Restrained by his fellows, he was later sent back to a psychiatric centre.

Protective devices

When in a state of 'protective' inhibition an individual seems to be in a stupor, he loses his memory and is unable to use arms or legs. Fainting attacks are common. Some sufferers become paralysed from fear, some succumb to nervous exhaustion, the latter usually being men of stable personality who have been both under mental stress and deprived of sleep and food for long spells.

Army psychiatrists noted that in certain cases the inhibition, the failure to act, was limited to certain areas of the brain. These areas controlled certain bodily activities, such as those of speech. So dumbness and stammering during the period of recovery from inhibition were very common. One patient stammered when he heard an officer call him a coward. Some patients with fixed, rigid faces complained of lumps in the throat; some with weak, bent backs were not completely paralysed in the legs, complete paralysis being uncommon, although walking was slowed down.

In other combat troops under treatment for stress, some of the areas of the brain were stimulated and others inhibited. In the same man there could be rigidity of facial movements or a stammer, together with severe tremors of hands and body or jerking movements. The upper part of the body might shake violently while the lower part remained motionless. A set or grinning face might be accompanied by jerking and writhing of other parts of the body.

According to Sargant, sudden changes from excitement to inhibition or the reverse were often seen in these soldiers. An order to attack caused one man, who was trembling and frightened in a ditch, to leap up and shout and then to faint when an officer called out to him 'A girl would put up a better show!' Other soldiers responding to stress situations ran about shouting in panic and then became suddenly dumb.

One patient, who had been subjected to severe bombing, was asked to hold out his hands as a test for tremor. He obeyed but was not then able to lower his hands when told until he transferred his thoughts to something else such as getting a cigarette from his pocket. Other patients reacted to severe stress by being unable to move however hard they tried. yet when they stopped trying their condition began to improve. Sargant points to a similarity in everyday life among brain-workers, who when under some stress due to overwork remember words or names when they stop trying to do so, although they cannot remember those details when they consciously try hard to recollect them.

A common reaction to the stress of bombing is loss of memory. At the time of Dunkirk and the blitz, civilian and military patients admitted to a London neurosis centre were afflicted by temporary loss of memory. In peace time a psychiatrist in unlikely to meet more than one or two cases of this nature in a year, yet in 1942 many hundreds of patients presented these symptoms. This loss of memory is a protective device, a simple inhibition imposed by the brain, which refuses to respond to overwhelming stress.

Loss of weight is another common reaction to stress. During the blitz patients who suffered from acute anxiety and other forms of neurosis were found to have lost as much as 15 to 30 lb. in weight.

Prisoners-of-war

The continuing effect of the body's stress response long after the stress situation had ceased to exist was noted earlier in the experience of industrial workers. These findings have been confirmed by studies done into the subsequent history of men who were prisoners-of-war in Japanese hands during World War II.

Dr Harold Wolff, an American who studied the effect of stress responses in individuals, paid particular attention to the time lag involved. In one research project he wanted to see if prisoners-of-war who had suffered severely in the hands of the enemy were affected long after they had returned to civilian life. He examined the case histories of twenty-five thousand American soldiers captured in the Pacific theatre of war. Many of these men were forced to work hard while at the same time being subjected to extreme humiliation, beatings, starvation and lack of medical attention at the hands of their Japanese captors. Of this number one-third died in captivity. Of the remainder the number of deaths that had occurred during the six years after the war ended was more than twice the death rate of people of the same age group who had not undergone prisoner-of-war experience, and three times as great as American prisoners-of-war captured in Europe and held in German prison camps.

Surprisingly the causes of death of the Pacific group of ex-prisoners did not relate to starvation as might have been expected. Cancer and heart disease claimed twice as many victims as from the normal population of the same age group, four times the normal number died from gastro-intestinal diseases, and as many as nine times the normal number from pulmonary tuberculosis. Twice the expected number committed suicide.

Among those who were still alive after six years the amount of chronic illness—hernia, deafness, diseases of heart, bones and muscles—was ten times as much as that suffered by prisoners-of-war in Europe.

Yet if the illnesses did not relate to the malnutrition and hardship suffered while in Japanese hands, what other causes could there have been? Research supports the view that organic illnesses need not necessarily be due to an organic cause; that it was the continuous response of the body to a series of stressful situations that had a long-term debilitating effect, leading to a number of illnesses that had no direct link with starvation.

11 *More Deliberate Stress: Interrogation*

Another man-made stress situation deliberately contrived to injure the individual exposed to it is interrogation. The aim of this procedure is to subject the prisoner to such a mental and physical battering that he 'confesses' to his captors, whatever the outcome of that confession may be. This type of interrogation has a long history, which credits the Catholic Inquisitors with its beginnings and Russian Communists with its ultimate refinements.

Broadly the aim is to induce tension, anxiety, mental exhaustion with physical debilitation, either singly or together so as to destroy the limit of normal brain function and resistance. In his detailed book which has become a standard work on the subject, *Battle for the Mind*, author William Sargant explains: 'To elicit confessions, one must try to create feelings of anxiety and guilt, to induce states of mental conflict if these are not already present. Even if the accused person is genuinely guilty, the normal function of his brain must be disturbed so that judgment becomes impaired.'

Once mental exhaustion is reached a victim of interrogation may either reject all his old doctrines and confess to something which is totally alien to his former beliefs or, alternatively, he is so open to suggestibility that he is prepared to admit guilt even though he is quite innocent. Nevertheless some individuals are able to resist the most persistent and sophisticated routines of questioning: Z. F. Stypulkowski's book *Invitation to Moscow* tells how he avoided making a confession despite over 130 periods of interrogation, which may be considered a rare achievement.

This merely confirms that we all have different limits of resistance and that what is an acute stress situation for one individual is not quite so acute for another. It is difficult to assess any one individual's reaction and resistance to physical pain; it is equally difficult to judge anyone's likely behaviour under interrogation. One thing is known, however—the mentally unstable are able to resist any examination.

The fictional idea of interrogation, where the unfortunate victim is faced by a bullying interrogator who shouts and threatens until the prisoner confesses all, is nonsense and the complete antithesis of the truth. While techniques may vary from regime to regime the basic purpose is always the same, to induce by every psychological means a total breakdown of the prisoner's mental resistance.

In fact Cyril Cunningham, who worked for many years as a forensic psychologist in a number of British government departments, and who is an expert on international interrogation techniques, says the idea of an interrogator engaging in a duel of wits is in reality an interrogator's nightmare and one which he hopes he will never have to face.

Background information

In areas as diverse as Northern Ireland, Russia, the United States, Korea and South Africa one prerequisite of all interrogations emerges—investigation of the prisoner's background, preferably without his knowledge, so that some 'weak spot' is discovered. Writing with particular reference to Northern Ireland and interrogations conducted with IRA suspects, Cunningham says that interrogation comprises three stages: 'The first is investigation, carried out by the interrogator or his agents usually *prior* to the arrest or detention of the suspect. It is a form of covert "questioning" since it may take place without the suspect's knowledge. Stage two is overt oral examination, commonly known as interrogation. However, interrogators do not cease probing when they stop talking. Hence stage three can be described as probing, and it consists of a range of secret techniques of surveillance, deception and decoy which are obviously never publicized.'

When the prisoner's 'skeletons in the cupboard' are unveiled it needs no imagination to realize what effect constant repetition and probing of this weak spot might have on someone whose liberty has already been forfeited, even temporarily.

The Long Kesh affair

However, if these practices seem comparatively gentlemanly, a government inquiry following parliamentary protests about British interrogation methods used on internees at Long Kesh camp, Northern Ireland, revealed a state of affairs sufficient to make Empire poet Sir Henry Newbolt ('play up, play up, and play the game!') turn several times in his grave. James Burke referred to these distinctly un-British methods of interrogation in a BBC television programme early in 1973. What is unusual about the Long Kesh affair is that a government commission of inquiry looked into it, and so provided an objective view of what can happen when interrogation takes place. According to the Compton Report, published in 1971 by the Home Office, internees had been made to stand for from four to six hours at a time, hands raised, facing a wall and leaning against it, their heads being covered with a hood so that they lost orientation with their surroundings. They were subjected to a continuous hissing noise or electronic 'mush'. One internee spent a total of 43½ hours being interrogated in this way. In addition, internees under interrogation were prevented from sleeping. The members of the committee of inquiry stated in the report: 'We consider that the following actions constitute physical ill-treatment; posture on the wall, hooding, noise, deprivation of sleep and diet of bread and water.'

The disclosure by the official inquiry that these practices were being employed by British Army Intelligence resulted in this particular interrogation technique being forbidden.

In the more orthodox interrogation procedures it should not

be assumed that the victim is an unwilling partner in a duel of wits. He is not constantly on his guard at all times in the face of his interrogator, merely denying all the accusations made or refusing to offer information required. On the contrary, he can be lured into a totally euphoric state simply by being reminded of things familiar and very personal to him in his everyday life. What could be more beguiling to any of us, especially in a state of tension, uncertainty and fear, than to talk to a friendly stranger of our family, friends and interests? In examining the known methods of criminal and political interrogation used in various countries the most familiar is that of the British police, who have the reputation of being the best-disciplined and fairest police force in the world. And yet in recent years, largely as a result of newspaper investigations, doubt has been expressed about the authenticity of some evidence produced in criminal trials in Britain.

Use of psychology

Nevertheless there are very strict limits to police powers of examination. Perhaps it is a tribute to the advances made in the application of psychology to interrogation that they seem almost enough to elicit the most surprising—and sometimes disturbing—confessions.

Experience has shown that the prisoner will make the most detailed statement just after he has been formally charged with the crime. According to William Sargant: 'Suspects, whether they have been arrested soon after the commission of the alleged crime, or whether only after frequent interrogations and a long period of suspense, are likely to be put into a highly anxious and emotional state when formally charged and to find the power of their brain temporarily disorganized. This is the precise point when a state of increased suggestibility . . . is most likely to occur; when, in fact, such persons may be most easily persuaded to make statements which not only increase their chances of conviction but even sometimes incriminate them unjustly.'

In the United States the police make much use of the lie-detector and claim they are justified in so doing, since as many as 80 per cent of people detained confess to crimes once they are shown by the machine to be guilty. Even in Russia, where the most extreme forms of interrogation are used, and the dangerous limits of psychological stress are sometimes over-reached, they still rely upon the need to disturb, confuse and finally break down mental resistance by discovering the sensitive area in the suspect's past history of which he is probably ashamed, or by which he is embarrassed or which he is afraid to have brought to light.

To quote a description of the kind of stress situation a prisoner in Stalin's Russia would be exposed to: 'Every effort was made to stir up anxiety, to implant guilt, to confuse the victim, to create a state in which he does not know what is going to happen to him from one minute to the next.' William Sargant's vivid account goes on: 'His diet was restricted to ensure loss of weight and debilitation; because physiological stimuli, which may fail when body weight is at its normal figure of, say, 140 lb., tend to produce rapid breakdown when body weight has dropped to about 90 lb. Every effort was also made to disrupt normal behaviour patterns. To begin with, the victim might be called from his work for questioning by the police, and then be ordered to resume it again and attend a further examination a few days later. Several such examinations might take place before his eventual arrest.'

Alexander Weissberg in his book *Conspiracy of Silence* has a bitter story to tell of first-hand experience of what it is like on the receiving end of this kind of mental torment. While being questioned before his actual arrest he reports: 'I went over the events of the last ten years in my mind. I considered everyone with whom I had been in personal contact, or with whom I had corresponded. And in the end I found nothing at all which could reasonably offer grounds for suspicion. . . . Suddenly, a long-forgotten incident which had taken place in 1933 came to my mind and what calmness I had left was utterly destroyed. My God! I thought. That must be it!'

As it happened it was a small incident totally unconnected with the crime alleged to have been committed by Weissberg, a

German Communist with the rare distinction of having gone through the treadmill of the Stalinist purge shortly before the last war and having survived. In fact Weissberg, after spending three years in Russian prisons, and being forced to sign confessions which he later withdrew, was repatriated to Germany under the Russo-German Treaty of 1939.

Abnormal states

Many types of stress situations can be constructed to induce abnormal states of brain activity. The ultimate object is the same, namely to wear down the victim by a process of physical debilitation until he is unable to exercise proper control over his mental functions.

A West German journalist captured and made to confess in an East German prison later told how he was kept awake for ten days. At night, lying under a bright electric light in his cell, he was awakened every fifteen minutes. Then, at regular fifteen-minute intervals, guards would pound on the cell door, there would be shrill whistling, flashing lights. Small wonder that after ten nights he was suffering from hallucinations and was considered by his captors to be about right for intensive interrogation.

The rather more subtle persuasive techniques of the American lie-detector are amply illustrated in a book *The Instrumental Detection of Deception* (1953) by Clarence D. Lee. Although written twenty years ago it does show that the machine is a very effective instrument that can be, in itself, a stress situation, in that both the experienced and the ignorant who are guilty respond to it by making confessions: 'The sight of the pens swinging to every heart-beat and breath may well shatter the morale. Showing him the recorded results, with a brief explanation of the significance of the different indices of deception, often will produce immediate results. Or pointing out the similarities between the reactions accompanying the single lie in a control test and [his] reactions to relevant questions in the formal test is likewise helpful. As a means of inducing confessions, any procedure of this type is permissible *after* the examiner is convinced of the subject's guilt through the prescribed methods of testing.'

The author makes a pronouncement: 'Those most susceptible to an appeal to the emotions are the easiest to induce to confess. In this group are the so-called accidental offenders, such as the hit-and-run offender, those who kill in the heat of passion, juveniles and first offenders, as well as the sex-offenders.'

Sympathetic interrogators

Even within the framework of a purely 'mechanical test' of the kind conducted with the aid of a lie-detector there is a shrewd psychological advantage on the side of the examiner.

Clarence Lee in his book explains: 'Where a sympathetic approach is indicated, it is well to play on the self-justification that is usually in the mind of the criminal for his misdeeds. Suggest that there was a good reason for his having committed the deed, that he has too much intelligence to have done it without rhyme or reason. In the case of sex crimes, explain that sex hunger is one of the strongest instincts motivating our lives. In case of theft, suggest that the subject may have been hungry, or deprived of the necessities of life; or in homicide, that the victim had done him a great wrong and probably had it coming to him. Be friendly and sympathetic and encourage him to write out or relate the whole story—to clean up and start afresh.'

If a prisoner appears to be weakening and looks like reciprocating some kind of feeling of affection for his interrogator, who may well have been treating him harshly a short time ago, then it is a sure sign he is at breaking-point.

Stypulkowski, who held out so long against his Stalinist interrogators, reports in his book *Invitation to Moscow* that at one stage his examiner, perhaps sensing that he was winning, and sensing too that the time was ripe to drop the mask of interrogator for that of father confesser, tells him: 'I am sorry for you. I see how tired you are. I am happy to inform you, on behalf of the authorities, that the Soviet Government has no wish you should lose your life, or spend thirty years rotting in some labour camp in Siberia. On the contrary, the Soviet Government wants you to live and work as a free man.'

It was a carefully timed and highly emotive appeal. Looking out of his prison cell window the unfortunate writer sees the dawn breaking, a new day with all the hope and promise of it awaiting him if he capitulates. Is holding out really worth it?

Breakdown under stress

The prisoner takes the bait, he rushes to tell the interrogator all he wants to know, anxious to convince him he is holding nothing back; he really wants to make a clean breast of everything.

Retrospectively, Stypulkowski is able to analyse the enormous consequences of his mental and physical breakdown. Describing his reactions and those of anyone else exposed to similar stress situations he says: 'In his determination to confess all, he talks about things that never happened, repeats gossip he once heard. It is still not enough for the examiner, so the prisoner tries to remember something more—just to prove conclusively he does not intend to conceal anything. The prisoner still relies on his intelligence, his critical powers and his character to guide him and restrict his depositions to harmless statements of fact. But here he is wrong. He does not realize that during the few weeks of questioning his faculties have become diminished, his power to reason has become corrupted. . . . he is a completely changed man.'

The commonest man-contrived stress situation that promotes anxiety and thus aids confession is the threat of torture. L. Fabre in his biography of Joan of Arc describes the situation in which the Maid of Orleans found herself: 'Monsieur de Beauvais gave her sufficient time to take in the nature of the assembled implements, the pulleys and cords, the winches and the rack, the malles and the funnels, the hooks, the gridirons, the knives, the spikes, the boot, the pincers, and the braziers glowing in the shadows . . .' Differing techniques, certainly, but both with the same elusive and sometimes difficult goal. To prize by every skill at the disposal of the interrogators the reluctant oyster from its shell.

Today in America equipment for brain-washing and interrogation, designed to create extreme stress for its victims, is on sale to 'official' customers, government departments and police forces from many countries all over the world.

As Drs J. S. Pippard and P. S. Greaves wrote to *The Lancet* in May 1973: 'One of the most deeply disturbing threats to human dignity and freedom in the past few decades has been the steadily growing use of torture as an instrument of policy in many countries which, on most other grounds, could claim to be civilized. . . .'

They went on to deplore the action of doctors who assisted in the evil work: '. . . we are most deeply concerned at the frequency with which reports of torture, endured or witnessed, have referred to medical men being involved in its administration. This involvement seems to have been confined usually to the assessment of the victim's capacity to undergo further torment, and to the administration of drugs as part of the deliberate aggravation of such suffering through sleep deprivation and other physiological means. All who have any part in the torturing of a human being are to be condemned unreservedly; but medical men and women have special obligations to alleviate suffering, and, whenever possible, to remove its causes, and, for that reason, are more to be condemned when they prostitute their professional skills in the infliction of torture upon another.'

In the USSR many psychiatrists disgrace their profession by collaborating in unethical practices. Writers who are critical of the regime are certified by these psychiatrists to be suffering from schizophrenia. Dissenters on political charges are thus effectively hospitalized in penal institutions without trial.

12 *Sudden Catastrophes*

War and interrogation subject the individual to continuous or periodic stress situations which in the course of time, and depending on the make-up of the individual, produce exhaustion from which severe illness or death can result. In contrast being involved in a natural disaster does not have this effect. If one had to forecast the outcome of research into the behaviour of people caught up in such catastrophes as hurricanes, severe flooding or earthquakes one would most likely have predicted panic and bodily and mental illness as a response to stress situations. Yet the reports published by the Ohio State University Disaster Research Center show that the opposite is the case. At the most a few dozen people were involved in panic behaviour in a twenty-year period of time.

More than a hundred natural disasters have been studied and the behaviour of the people involved investigated by the Center. The results topple generally held beliefs about what happens when disaster strikes an area. First, there is practically no panic. The idea of panic is a myth, built up over the years by press, radio and television with their selective reporting of incidents and over-estimates of injury and death. Some reporters believe the myth; they carry a mental image of what should happen in a disaster and they are liable to report what they imagine has happened.

The Disaster Research Center cites one instance in America of the situation that arose in 1961 when the hurricane Carla swept across Texas and Louisiana. More than half a million people left their homes in the path of the hurricane before it arrived. There were no deaths as the orderly evacuation took place, and less than 1 per cent of the evacuees were involved in traffic accidents along the route. Yet several newspapers carried a 'More than 100,000 people flee in near-panic' type of headline.

In Britain we cling to the story that there was panic in the streets of America the night that the Orson Welles's radio production of *The War of the Worlds*, dealing with an invasion by men from Mars, went out over the air. Yet a survey has shown that 84 per cent of the audience remained undisturbed throughout the programme. There are many other examples in the records of the Disaster Research Center of entirely unfounded reports of panic following communal disasters.

The positive aspect of the behaviour of people involved is underlined by the Center's findings. Disaster victims show themselves quite capable of handling rescue operations, except where medical aid or special lifting and cutting equipment is required. In the Michigan tornado disaster of 1953 there were 927 casualties, and almost three-quarters of them were taken to hospital within four hours of the tornado striking. This was done almost entirely without help from official organizations.

Morale high

Such disasters are in themselves stress situations and call forth bodily responses from the people involved. They are also situations in which the body is keyed up, full of energy *and is able to take positive action*. Unlike repetitive stress situations brought about by low-flying aircraft that are endured, say, by Heathrow residents, in which no positive action can be taken, the stress response in a natural disaster finds expression in seeking help from relatives and friends or in giving help to other sufferers. And then, working together to rescue the injured and to clear away debris, a feeling of communal solidarity is created, which effectively breaks down class and racial barriers. All the evidence collected by the Disaster Research Center points to the fact that in natural disasters the morale of the general public is high.

These findings confirm the experience of many who went through the London blitz during World War II.

And, as in the whole of Britain in the war years, mental illness declined. It is the exception for disaster victims to break down, mentally or physically, as a result of the body's response to the stress situation. Medical records and details of hospital admissions show that following a natural communal disaster there is a drop in the number of admissions to mental hospitals and in the number of out-patients at psychiatric clinics.

So, for the great majority of those involved, taking positive action in association with others uses up the fight or flight energy that is called up by the body's response to stress. It is a simple, straightforward situation; something needs to be done and the body provides the energy to do it.

Only a minority—about 10 per cent—do not show this positive reaction in communal disasters. Some of these display an extreme form of apathy and a regression of normal thought processes. This underlines the differing responses of individuals; people who form this minority have been caught up in a stress response so acute and immediate that the individual's physical and mental functioning is thrown out of balance. In so doing they throw into greater relief the positive reaction of the great majority.

Even at Hiroshima—where the dropping of the atom bomb in 1945 led to the greatest man-made communal disaster in history—although most of the survivors fled their flight could not be termed panic. After the blast and destruction there came the belief, commonly held in most disasters, that they had lived through the worst. Unaware of the dangers of fall-out and its lingering deadly effect, they returned to the city. The flight from the city was the right thing to do; it was what psychologists call an adaptive response, for those who did not flee were killed by the very rapid spread of fire.

Only one incident of panic has been verified. It occurred when a crowd of people, whose only way of escape was towards a river, were pressed closer and closer to its banks by the heat of the flames approaching them on three sides, and a number of people closest to the river's edge were pushed in and drowned.

The support provided by the community, and the feeling that one is not alone in the new and difficult-to-comprehend situation, are factors in maintaining high morale and a high degree of immunity from illness in community disasters.

Death in the family

But there are catastrophes that happen that are not shared with others, that one has to face alone. Such is bereavement, an experience everyone is likely to undergo at one time or another. Bereavement is a form of social stress stemming from a person's relationship with another. It calls forth a physical response from the body, although the realization that death has occurred is entirely a mental process.

This is a stress situation in which no action can be taken, in contrast to the response to the catastrophes mentioned above.

Far more attention needs to be paid to this type of stress situation, which produces in the body a response we call Grief. What are the symptoms? Dr G. Engel, an American psychiatrist, in an article entitled 'What is Grief?' in the magazine *Psychosomatic Medicine* (1961) describes it as follows: 'Generally it includes an initial phase of shock and disbelief in which the sufferer attempts to deny the loss and to inhibit himself against the shock of reality. This is followed by a stage of developing awareness of the loss, marked by the painful effects of sadness, guilt, shock, helplessness or hopelessness; by a sense of loss and emptiness, by anorexia, sleep disturbances, sometimes somatic symptoms of pain or other discomfort, loss of interest in one's usual activities and associates, impairment of work performance. Finally there is a prolonged phase of restitution and recovery during which the work of mourning is carried on. The trauma of the loss is overcome, and a state of health and well-being is established.'

Bereavement is an experience which few people know how to cope with. They neither know how to handle the bewildering emotions, nor what to expect from others, nor what others expect from them. All this is brought out in a book entitled *Grief*, the 'report' by Sarah Morris of her own experience of mourning. Her book is perhaps the only layman's account of grief and how to cope with it that is easily available to the public.

According to Sarah Morris sufferers go through three stages. The first is one of shock; this is probably the one which the bereaved find hardest to bear. So disturbing is it that some feel that they are becoming mentally unstable, for their behaviour is abnormal. In fact acting abnormally at this time is part of the normal pattern of the first stage. One sufferer, says Sarah Morris, might feel choked, short of breath. Another might experience nausea and so great a fatigue as to be unable to walk. One bereaved person described her feeling as like being deprived of a lung, and so found it extremely difficult to walk, talk or move.

Stage one usually lasts until after the funeral. Then the second stage is reached, the most important, when 'the work of mourning', as it is called by psychiatrists, has to be done. This is an extremely painful process. In it the emotional ties with the past and the hopes for the future that still link the bereaved with the deceased are broken. Hurtful reminders of the loss should not be pushed aside by the bereaved, but should be dwelt on. Writing and talking to people about the deceased helps with the work. In time—and the length of time differs with the individual, it can be weeks, months, even years—there will be periods when the hurt does not seem so great. Slowly the bereaved person is able to get free of painful memories and can begin to get involved and take an interest in other matters.

There are other stresses brought about by bereavement as well as that experienced through grief. Margaret Torrie in her book *Begin Again* discusses the effect of the death of a husband, and the ways in which the widow can deal with her bereavement on a practical and social level as well as an emotional one. She took an invaluable step towards providing help when she founded the organization Cruse, a counselling service for widows and their children. She makes a suggestion in her book that cardiologists might do well to consider. This is that heart disease, so much more prevalent among men than women, may be caused in part by the failure of men to respond to pain and grief by crying. 'There was a time,' she says, 'not so long ago when men in this country could weep publicly and not be discredited.' If she is right the stiff upper lip may not, after all, be so admirable a practice.

Bereavement is an example of an outside event that cannot be seen to inflict physical damage as a blow would, yet it calls forth a stress response just as great as direct physical injury. In a semi-rural area in Wales a GP, Dr Dewi Rees, conducted an investigation into the effect of bereavement on health. He found that nearly 5 per cent of bereaved close relatives died within a year of their bereavement, compared with 0.7 of the non-bereaved control group. The figures for those who had lost a spouse were even higher—12 per cent compared with 1 per cent in the control group.

New forms of ritual needed

The decay of convention increases the number of stress situations arising out of bereavement. Convention implies that everyone knows how to behave in certain circumstances, and without the convention many people are at a loss. Now that much of the ritual surrounding death and burial is disappearing, friends encountering the bereaved person soon after the bereavement are often in a dilemma whether or not to offer sympathy or how to offer it. Only among orthodox Jews is there an established ritual that recognizes the need for mourning, and for community support for that mourning through a prescribed period of time.

The decay of mourning conventions is regrettable, for as has been said the stress response brought on by death in the family can be severe, and those most affected need all the support they can get from friends. Heartfelt grief can be likened to a physical illness. People suffering from it cannot be expected to 'snap out of it' any more than they can be expected to resume work immediately after an operation.

Dr Eric Lindemann, an American psychiatrist writing in the

American Journal of Psychiatry, 1944, said in his article 'Symptomatology and Management of Acute Grief' that the length of time that suffering is felt depends on the success with which the bereaved person readjusts to the environment from which the deceased is now missing, and forms new friendships: 'The duration of a grief reaction seems to depend upon the success with which a person does the *grief work*, namely emancipation from the bondage of the deceased, readjustment to the environment in which the deceased is missing, and the formation of new relationships. One of the big obstacles to this work seems to be the fact that many bereaved people try to avoid the intense distress connected with the grief experience, and to avoid the expression of emotion necessary for it.'

With the decay of ritual surrounding death, society has little to offer the bereaved. Close friends should be helping him or her to give expression to grief and so to 'work through' the distress, for otherwise the recovery may be delayed and perhaps never properly achieved. But at this point in time, when new thinking about death and mourning is greatly needed, these friends are often mute, unable to help.

The professional undertakers are disliked for their mercenary approach to their business. To the great majority of people—non-church goers—the funeral services are meaningless and an embarrassment to be endured. We are looking for new ways of expressing grief, new ways of paying respect to the dead. The old ways, based on religious belief, are now for the most part irrelevant and an embarrassment to all taking part. This in itself is sufficient to set up a stress response in mourners.

Speaking to the British Medical Association meeting in 1973, Dr Murray Parkes, a psychologist of the Tavistock Institute of Human Relations, suggested that there should be preparation for bereavement.

He said that women should face the fact that they were likely to become widows. Although the mind boggled at the thought of 'widowhood courses', something could be done to get people used to that type of stress.

'People are often quite unprepared for the death of husbands, wives, parents and others these days, but a hundred years ago every child could expect to lose one brother or sister, every mother could expect to lose one of her children. Nowadays it is possible to live much of one's life without seeing anyone die or experiencing a major bereavement.'

Speaking on the effects of bereavement, he said parents could prepare the children for it by leaving the dead goldfish floating in the bowl for them to see; by letting them conduct a funeral service on the passing of the family cat or dog; and by not condemning it as 'morbid' if the children were seen poring over the death of Beth in *Little Women*.

There was evidence that extremely young children who were gravely distressed when their parents died were more likely to grow up to be potential suicides or dependent on tranquillizers and psychiatrists.

Stress and surgery

Another situation that is often seen as a catastrophe is the need for an operation. Mr Lipkin was on probation for stealing socks from Woolworths. He was employed as a typesetter at a small printing works. The offence happened when he was having a day off from work because his piles were giving him trouble. Every month he had three or four days off; they were isolated from each other, so that he could not claim sickness benefit, and with his family commitments he could not make ends meet. He got into the habit of going into big stores and stealing small items—socks, toothpaste, soap—what he called 'the essentials'. He made it clear that he never stole luxuries, only those things the family needed to maintain a minimum standard of living.

One of the first things I did, with Mr Lipkin's permission, was to contact his GP to discuss the man's physical condition. It transpired that the doctor had strongly recommended surgery for the piles; Mr Lipkin had just as firmly refused. Going through his early history with me, he told me the reason why he declined to have the operation. As a boy of ten he had had his tonsils removed. That nightmare was still with him; the crudity of the operation, the lack of sympathy shown by the doctor, the blood, the pain, the crying of the other children. No more operations for him if he could help it.

This hard-line attitude was changed by a quite exceptional act of consideration on the part of the hospital surgeon. Approached by the GP, he saw Mr Lipkin at the hospital, discussed with him in some detail the operation, showed him either by a diagram or model what wanted to be done and how it would be done. Mr Lipkin was even shown the ward he would be admitted to, and he met the ward sister. The operation was performed. In a few months, freedom from the pain of piles made him a changed man.

He told me that before the operation he was very anxious and indeed frightened. But he had confidence in the surgeon, and felt too that after the kindness he had been shown he could not let the hospital down by refusing to be operated on.

Until 1960 very little interest had been shown in this country in the stress response induced by the prospect of surgery, but as a result of an investigation by Dr Pamela Briskin in twenty surgical wards of nine London hospitals, involving more than 350 patients, it was demonstrated that the prospect of undergoing an operation provoked very strong emotions in most people.

This may seem obvious, but the existence of a stress response in patients had formerly been largely ignored by hospital authorities. As Dr Briskin puts it: 'More likely the reason for reluctance to inquire into the emotional concomitants of surgery may be a professional blind spot, conveniently closing official eyes from viewing further complications to an already complex and dangerous calling.'

The research showed that measures taken by the hospitals to deal with the anxiety and fear of patients awaiting surgery were quite inadequate. In particular it came out that people having an operation for the first time and those who could be described as 'neurotic' were much more likely to feel extreme anxiety than others. Women on the whole were more able to express their feelings of alarm and despair than men, but this did not mean that men did not experience those feelings.

There was also evidence—and this was paralleled by Mr Lipkin's case history—that traumatic experiences in the past connected with doctors and hospitals led to negative, hostile and helpless feelings. It became clear that everything that hospital doctors did or said—or did not say—was analysed by the patient and often found to hold dire tidings. The sound 'tch, tch, tch' made by a doctor was interpreted as a sentence of death, silence was taken to mean 'there's no hope' or 'it's gone too far', or 'they can't tell me because it's too bad'.

What is obviously necessary is that it should be recognized by medical staff that anxiety exists in patients, and that the personality of doctors and nurses, and the interest they show in patients, play a most important part in creating confidence and relieving anxiety. Abruptness, unkindness, arrogance or indifference expressed by doctors or nurses increase the patient's depression and fears.

Adding to the burden of the handicapped

That a handicapped person finds himself caught up in a chronic stress situation does not have to be emphasized. A physical or mental handicap is a catastrophe both for the individual and his or her family.

What so frequently happens in our society is that we add to the force of the stress in a number of ways.

First, for the sufferer whose disability is not present at birth, but arises out of illness or accident, a stressful experience lies in wait when he finally realizes that he will never be able to live a normal life again. This situation raises the question of the extent to which doctors should be frank with their patients. According to one researcher, when the patient does learn the truth of his condition a period of shock follows. As a rule the younger the patient the greater the shock. To delay this shock the physician often decides not to divulge the facts. He tries to soften the blow. Almost inevitably the patient becomes uncertain about the future.

He tries to learn the situation by questioning nurses and relatives. Sometimes his hopes are raised by the explanations which are given to him, but then when these hopes do not come to fruition, a period of depression sets in which can make the basic complaint even worse. Many physicians now follow a course which gives factual information to the patient and do not attempt to raise false hopes. This is accompanied by some form of supportive therapy to help cushion the shock and to help the patient to adjust to the situation. This means putting forward a goal towards which the patient can strive, something within his range, a realizable ambition, both in his private life and in his future occupation.

Secondly, the frustration felt by many physically handicapped people is heightened in this country by economic pressures. A few years ago the Disablement Income Group Charitable Trust reported that Britain's 1,500,000 disabled are among the most shabbily treated in Europe. The trust conducted a survey of benefits paid to the disabled in Britain, France, West Germany, the Netherlands, Denmark, Norway and Sweden. Britain is the only country that does not have a pension for the disabled apart from those whose disability resulted from the war or industrial accident.

Most of us are familiar with the way in which such well-known individuals as Franklin D. Roosevelt, Douglas Bader, Michael Flanders and Lady Masham have shown courage and perseverance in coping with physical handicap. There are others whose achievements make news—competitors in the Olympic Games for Paraplegics or the young man with artificial legs who climbed Tryfan in Snowdonia, doing the last stretch in deep snow on all fours. These people serve to remind us that the handicapped have the same human needs—and often can satisfy them—as their more fortunate fellows.

Thirdly, the physically handicapped have to cope with stress situations that arise not only out of their own particular handicap but also out of the reaction of other people to it. If we examine closely the problems of someone with a minor handicap (though major to the sufferer), such as a person who stammers, it is likely that a double handicap will be present, both the stammer and other people's attitude towards it.

On probation to me was Richard, whose father, an ex-sergeant-major, expected implicit obedience from his family. He got it, generally by shouting. Surprisingly Richard, who was the middle child of three sons, was the only one who opposed him; a particularly difficult feat because the boy had so pronounced a stammer that it was embarrassing at times to watch his struggle to emit a word. At our first meetings I found myself supplying the missing word. It was a senior probation officer who, being present at one interview, said to me afterwards: 'Does he like you filling in the gaps for him?' Frankly I did not know. At our next interview I mentioned this to Richard and he said he did not like my providing the word when he was in difficulties. He explained that he had the word all ready to come out and if I supplied it (or one which I thought he intended to use) it caused him to lose the impetus he needed to get the phrase out.

Douglas Bader is on record as saying that in the early days of his disability he was determined to be completely independent of other people and not to accept help in walking or carrying articles. Today he asks for help when it is needed and finds this is a good way of carrying on and one that saves embarrassment. If he walks uphill on a golf course he asks his partner to give him a pull up; when going downhill he finds it is better to cling on to someone's arm.

This determination to be independent is common with handicapped people who wish to do everything they can for themselves. It is only later when they are able to accept the situation that they are also able to accept other people's help, although for some the help of others is always needed.

And how does it affect the family of a handicapped person? They are under continual strain. In particular, parents of handicapped children respond as they would to any other stress situation. For some the body's repeated response to stress in time leads to breakdown.

Mr and Mrs Young had four children, the eldest son being epileptic. This boy's condition could be controlled by drugs. As he grew older he found that he could use his handicap as a form of blackmail to get his own way. He demanded more pocket money than the others, declined to do any small job such as running errands for his parents, and stayed away from school almost at will.

He refused to take his tablets unless he was allowed to do as he wished. When he did not take his prescribed dosage he would either have an epileptic seizure or become so aggressive that all the family became afraid of him. On several occasions he stole from neighbours, increasing the strain on his parents, who felt keenly the disgrace their son had brought on them. Eventually Mr Young deserted his family, leaving his wife to cope as best she could. He was frank in admitting that he was at fault, but insisted that it was in 'self-defence'—if he had not got away he would have had a mental breakdown.

This was an exceptional instance. The majority of parents—with considerable financial and physical sacrifice—centre their lives on the handicapped child, to give the youngster as near normal a life as possible. It is on record that one lorry driver who had a thalidomide son spent more than £1,000 (his life savings) on machines and equipment to improve the quality of his son's life. When that money was gone he obtained a bank overdraft, sold his car and gave up tobacco and alcohol to keep up the provision of those things which he regarded as essential for his child. Many of the parents of the thalidomide children gave up work, many had to change their houses to go into bungalows, many have been reduced almost to penury thanks to the dilatory behaviour of the Distillers Company.

The stress response to such a situation takes its toll in physical and mental ill health. The thalidomide affair brought home to the public the suffering not only of the children but of their parents in the ten years they had to struggle without adequate financial help.

The effect on the parents was dealt with by Dr Gerard

Vaughan, MP for Reading, when the House of Commons debated the plight of the thalidomide children in December 1972. In the course of his practice he had examined sixty of the children whose cases had at that time appeared before the courts. He said: 'I should like now to mention the families. Some of them have broken up, some of them have drawn together. It is relevant that we in this country have kept 90 per cent of the children at home, whereas in Germany most of them have gone into institutions. But every one of the mothers of those sixty children is ill, taking tranquillizers for her nerves, and has done so virtually continuously since her thalidomide child was born.

'We are dealing here not just with parents of handicapped children but with parents who are themselves under great stress and difficulty.'

13 Coping with Stress

Mrs Lloyd applied to the magistrates for the custody of three children of the marriage. On learning of the circumstances leading to the application the court adjourned the hearing and asked the probation officers to try to bring about a reconcilation between wife and husband.

Mr and Mrs Lloyd formerly lived in a small village just outside a large industrial city. It was the village where the wife had always lived, and where her parents and brothers and sisters still resided. Mr Lloyd spent a number of years attending evening classes at the technical college in order to gain professional qualifications. With these qualifications he had obtained a much better job in London.

The family moved to the capital. In the new home Mrs Lloyd, a woman with a shy, retiring manner, was very unhappy. She had always relied on her parents and brothers and sisters to provide the social contacts she needed. In the new environment she was quite unable to make friends, and she hated the crowds and traffic. Finally she left her husband and returned with the children to the village.

She frankly admitted that the marriage breakdown was her fault; she had nothing but good to say about her husband. Finally she agreed to return to London after the probation officer for the area had enlisted the support of a few people who promised to do what they could to make Mrs Lloyd feel more at home in the community. Even so, she returned to her home village again six months later, and once again agreed to rejoin her husband provided that her mother would live with them for three months.

It was not until the Lloyd family had been in London for four years that the wife felt she was finally settled there. This experience was such that Mr Lloyd dare not risk applying for another job in another town unless a vacancy happened to turn up in his native city. He had to be content to wait for promotion to come to him in the London branch of the organization.

Some people can adapt to change more readily than others. Mrs Lloyd was not one of these. The quiet village where she was born and brought up, the small circles of family and friends, the seeming absence of change—or change so slow as to be almost imperceptible—is what she asked from life. She did not realize her dislike of change until she was forced into it. Her inability to adapt to it then produced so much stress response in her that it almost broke up the marriage.

It was not just the move from one house to another, or the slow process of making new friends. City life was so much more crowded, hurried, noisy and anonymous than that of the village. It is these additional factors present in urban living that create stress in town-dwellers. Recently the State of New York published statistics which showed that mental disorders of all kinds were twice as great in the city as in rural areas, and there was a greater incidence of ulcers in town than in country.

In towns in Britain the overcrowding, found especially in the poorer suburbs, is linked with schizophrenia. Areas of London like Stepney and Stoke Newington, whose overcrowding is high, have a schizophrenia discharge rate from psychiatric hospitals of around 20 per 1,000 people. Less densely populated areas like Wood Green and Edmonton have a rate ranging between 7 and 11 per 1,000. The Psychiatric Rehabilitation Association states that by looking at social conditions in a specific area it is possible to predict the number of schizophrenia patients. That heredity plays a part in the disease is not doubted, but there is an interaction between the make-up of the potential schizophrenic and his overcrowded—and therefore stress-laden—environment that causes the illness.

Lessening the impact

Several lines of action are open to us if we wish to lessen the harm done by the body's response to near-continuous stress situations.

First, we can reduce the amount of stress situations to which we are exposed by changing the environment that produces the stress.

Secondly, we can consider what stress situations we are creating for other people and so take decisions which do not give rise to stress situations. In this way the amount of stress in society is lessened.

Thirdly, we can change ourselves so that situations that formerly threatened us no longer do so.

The majority of people do none of these things. They neither oppose those factors in society which increase stress, nor do they train themselves to lessen the impact of stress situations by controlling their response to them. Instead they try to alleviate the almost continuous stress situations of everyday living by smoking, drinking and by using drugs that are obtainable without a doctor's prescription—aspirin, paracetamol, codeine and the like.

There are, of course, stress situations that produce such an acute bodily response that medical help has to be sought to relieve the anxiety and depression.

Here is an account by a married woman of the help she received from a course of drug therapy lasting nearly five years:

'In 1968, after a breakdown in my marriage and an attempted suicide (overdose of aspirin), my doctor suggested treatment in the form of drugs (librium). The dose was one tablet 3 times a day and this continued for six months, and then it was one tablet twice a day for another year, and for a further 2 years I had one tablet of librium once a day. By the time I reached 2 tablets of librium daily, I had begun to feel life worth living again, but whenever I tried leaving off librium I began to get depressions and so had to keep on with them. Until recently I have always kept the librium bottle handy, but can now say that in the spring of 1973 I am entirely without need of them.'

The annual number of prescriptions in the United Kingdom for anxiety-relieving drugs gives some indication of the increase in acute stress situations in recent years. In the ten years 1961 to 1971 they rose from 32.2 million to 47.8 million a year. In considering these figures we should remember that without the aid of such drugs many of the patients would either be dead or mentally ill. As it is, the vast majority—like the married woman quoted—are able to cope with their problems and remain active members of society while gradually reducing their dependence on the drug.

Changing the environment

We know the benefits to be obtained from moving out of an environment that produces too much stress. The week-end drive into the country, the search for a peaceful holiday spot, even the retreat into the garden or allotment demonstrate that we possess an instinctive knowledge of what kind of environment is low on stress.

Yet for town-dwellers this relief from environmental stress can only be sought intermittently; they cannot get away permanently from the place in which they live and work. Stress in this everyday environment can only be lessened by political action, action directed to ensure that decisions affecting our lives are judged from the viewpoint of human and not money values. An obvious example of stress situations being multiplied is the increase in size (and number) of road juggernauts referred to in Chapter 5. This increase is likely to continue since there is no integrated national freight-carrying policy that would get the heavy stuff off the roads and back on to the railways and canals. It might raise the cost of food to restrict lorry traffic but, as Hugh Dykes MP pointed out in a recent 'Man Alive' television programme, the consumer has never been asked which he would prefer; he has had the noise and stench foisted on him.

For those who believe that the motor-car is the major social problem of the day an obvious way of attempting to reduce its contribution to environmental stress is to join organizations such as the Pedestrians' Association for Road Safety—to which many motorists belong—or the Royal Society for the Prevention of Accidents, which directs part of its efforts to reducing road casualties.

Protest is good for you

One of the healthier aspects of society in recent years has been the growth of the various protest movements, a growth which is both a criticism of the existing state of parliamentary and local government democracy and a reaction to their shortcomings.

Those changes in the environment that produce stress instead of alleviating it ought not to be introduced without full consultation with the community that has to tolerate the stress situations created by the change. Yet how often does consultation take place?

When Westway was being built in West London no effort was made to rehouse some of the people of North Kensington who lived alongside the motorway. Day and night for months on end they endured the noise and dirt of roadworks, earthmovers, heavy lorries and mud. The physical stress was increased by mental stress in the knowledge that those who planned the motorway cared little. Peaceful requests for rehousing brought no response. Only illegal action, an organized protest which blocked the motorway when Westway was officially opened, gained a token victory over the indifference of officials. The subsequent publicity forced the planners to retreat from their previous policy of 'no help', and the long-suffering residents were rehoused.

Membership of protest movements such as conservation societies, motorway and airport opposition groups can be of benefit to health not only in the results achieved but also for their effect on the body. The pent-up energy of the 'fight or flight' mechanism that cannot be used in immediate direct action can be sublimated and made the mainspring for sustained effort.

The frustration and anger created in many people first in the Stansted, Essex, and then in the Cublington, Buckinghamshire, area by the announcement that London's third airport was to be built there, found an outlet in organizing two of the most successful protest movements in recent years.

Membership of a protest group has other beneficial side-effects in addition to using up the stress response energy. The gregarious instinct in man is satisfied, the feeling of 'belonging', of working together for a common cause, is stimulating, and the objective provides an aim in life which some people feel they lack.

Changing our life style

Secondly, if we are determined to lessen the dangers inherent in the overload of stress situations we can change our life style. Such a change can reduce either environmental or social stress situations or both. We can seek a less hectic physical environment by moving from urban to rural surroundings. Some people try to make the best of both worlds by living in the country and working in the town, but in travelling daily from one environment to another they may encounter new stress situations which leave the net result largely unchanged.

To reduce substantially the number of environmental stress situations one would have to make a definite break with urban living. This could be achieved, say, by the head teacher of a city comprehensive school taking over the headship of a small village school, recognizing that a cut in salary is inevitable in such a move.

It takes courage to do this, and even more to live up to the cliché and opt out of the rat race. It demands the deliberate choice of a much lower standard of living. It calls for a rejection of the values of the acquisitive society that equates social status with possessions, and so motivates people to strive for more and more money, even though there is a price to be paid in health. According to Ivor Mills, professor of medicine at Cambridge, the strain and worry of trying to earn more money to 'keep up with the Joneses' can make men impotent. This is just part of the price paid by some of us.

The search for a less stress-laden environment can be conducted as an end in itself or complementary to an attempt to reduce social stress situations. Personal relationships in any sphere of activity—home, work, leisure—produce many more threatening situations than even the most polluted and noisy environment, and yet it is easier to reduce social stress. Much of environmental stress is outside the immediate control of the individual. We cannot hope to lessen our financial worries by cutting the cost of living 'at a stroke'. A man cannot reduce the noise level of the factory where he is employed unless he is first prepared to work for months or years to bring about an improvement through trade union action. Almost any kind of environmental change is a long-term project; some of the difficulties in reducing factory noise were noted in a report by Sheffield acoustical experts, R. J. McConnell and Associates, published in May 1973, which said that factory noise is gradually deafening over half of Britain's workers in heavy industry. The report stated that employers are mostly to blame, but that some of the damage is due to the carelessness of workers in not using the issued protectives, and that trade unions are not aware of the dangers of excessive noise.

To get employers to do their share in improving conditions, to persuade workers to use protective equipment and to alert trade unions to the harmful effect of noise, are very desirable but nevertheless long-term objectives. A reduction in environmental stress achieved through them will take months or years.

Insight into behaviour

However, it is possible to reduce more quickly the social stress situations that arise out of our interaction with other people. With insight into our emotions, attitudes and motivations, gained through a study of psychology, we can modify our behaviour and even effect a change in behaviour patterns. What is needed by some is a switch from the A to B type as designated by two famous American cardiologists, Meyer Friedman and Ray H. Rosenman.

Friedman and Rosenman were forced by their researches to the conclusion that people show two major types of behaviour pattern, which they call A and B. Here are some of their characteristics:

Type A	*Type B*
Intense drive	More easy-going than A
Aggressive	Hard to make angry
Very ambitious	Not preoccupied with achievement
Highly competitive	Less competitive than A
Tendency to pit himself against the clock	Does not feel driven by the clock
Tremendously hard worker	Takes more time than A to enjoy leisure
Visibly restless	Seldom becomes impatient
A perfectionist	A reasonable man
Smokes cigarettes, not a pipe	Likely to smoke a pipe
Has an air of hostility which makes people nervous	Hard to make angry
Full of brisk, decisive self-confidence	Speaks in a modulated style
Does not linger over meals	Makes mealtimes social occasions
Often hard to get along with	Sociable
Often goes to bed early, not much time for socializing	Will stay up late either socializing or occupied with something irrelevant to his career

Many thousands of men in the age group thirty-nine to fifty-nine, with no known history of heart disease, were interviewed in 1960 at the outset of the research and were designated type A or B. Equal numbers of the two types, totalling 3,500, were then given complete physical examinations, which have continued throughout the research. Since the commencement of the study 257 of the test groups have developed coronary heart disease, of which 70 per cent have been type A. Obviously anyone who recognizes in himself characteristics of type A should strive to alter his life style.

The social stress situations encountered (mostly of type A's own making) are not confined to the world of work. Because they have little time for anything but the job, A-type people neglect their families. So they lose out on the satisfactions and emotional security which good family relationships provide, at the same time creating more social stress situations within the family circle.

Dr Rosenman is inclined to believe that not only does living in the type A style produce heart disease—the whole type A condition is a disease in itself although not yet recognized as such. Based on his research into the chemistry of stress reactions Dr Malcolm Carruthers of St Mary's Hospital, London, described in his book *The Western Way of Death* just how life in a competitive consumer society can cause heart attacks; much of his work confirms the Rosenman thesis.

Meeting life with meditation

A method gaining acceptance as a means of reducing the effect of stress situations is transcendental meditation, or the science of creative intelligence as its followers prefer to call it. Mantra meditation has hitherto been practised in a very complex form in some Eastern religions, and it is only in recent years that it has been introduced, using much simpler methods, into the West.

These methods take up some twenty minutes night and morning, during which time the meditator sits with closed eyes and concentrates on a sound—the mantra—which he repeats (silently) in his consciousness.

There have been several scientific investigations into the bodily effects achieved by this form of meditation, including research carried out at the Maudsley Hospital in London. It has been established that a reduction takes place in the level of arousal of the autonomic nervous system which controls the involuntary activities of the body, including heart rate and the amount of lactic acid in the blood. Normally a high level of autonomic activity and a high amount of lactic acid in the blood are linked with a high level of anxiety.

In the United States there have been dramatic decreases in the use of hard drugs when addicts became meditators. This has led the Public Health Service and the US Army to give financial support to projects studying meditation. Among non-drug takers many who currently practise transcendental meditation claim to be more relaxed and happier than they were before, and better able to cope with stress situations.

Gestalt therapy

Other forms of psychotherapy have been referred to earlier. One which is not so well known is Gestalt therapy. The techniques employed have their roots in the work of the late Dr Frederick Perls and the Esalen Institute at Big Sur, California.

Gestalt therapy does not preoccupy itself, as Freud did, with the burden of the past. Instead it is concerned with the here and now of everyday life, and in particular with making the individual aware of his behaviour, his tone of voice, gestures, facial expression and so on. Through this awareness comes self-knowledge which releases and sustains creativity, creativity that exists within every individual and should enhance his relationships with other people.

Many social stress situations produce ill health because the body's response is not allowed to express itself. When an employee gets a memo hinting at future redundancies the alarm sets off the 'fight or flight' response in his body. But there is no action he can take which will use up this energy. In modern life such an occurrence is not occasional but frequent, and every time it leaves what the Gestalt therapists call 'unfinished business' behind. Gestalt therapy aims to release this energy into creative channels and so reduce the effect of the body's stress response.

In America therapists who practise Gestalt principles are the third largest school of psychotherapy in the country. In Britain, as yet, its followers are not numerous.

Stress-producing actions

The third method of reducing stress is seen not from the viewpoint of the individual taking the action but from that of people whose lives are affected by it. In this field of activity the decisions of a relatively few people can produce severe stress situations for hundreds of others. So awareness of what certain decisions involve in terms of human happiness or anxiety is essential if unnecessary stress situations are to be avoided. This is a responsibility that devolves on all who plan community measures or have power over numbers of others. Their work can lessen or increase both environmental and social stress. Here are examples, some affecting small numbers of people, others affecting thousands.

Within the education system a greater emphasis on child psychology is needed in the curriculum of teachers in training, both to reduce stressful situations in schools and to help pinpoint those children who are displaying symptoms of maladjustment. It would also reduce, one hopes, the number of instances where pressure on parents to conform to school rules is exercised through the child so that the child endures the stressful situation.

Press reports of incidents in Bristol local authority schools highlighted this type of situation early in 1973, but similar examples could be found all over the country. A schoolgirl whose parents could not afford to buy her regulation sports kit for school games was made to walk around the playing field picking up litter while the rest of the class played hockey and netball. Then she had to write an essay on the importance of physical education. The teacher tore it up in front of the class without even reading it.

One boy, aged twelve, was told that he could not play cricket unless he had white flannels. His mother had to bleach a pair of old jeans until they were 'almost white'. A boy aged fifteen, whose parents could not afford sports kit, stayed at home on games days rather than face a beating with a plimsoll for not having the kit.

Housing

We have only to look at the housing situation to be aware that many local authorities allow houses to stand empty for years because some planned development is delayed, although there are hundreds of homeless families within that local authority's boundaries. Indeed there have been examples of local authorities deliberately smashing all the fitments in such houses to prevent homeless people from moving in as a temporary expedient. These stress situations caused by homelessness have been increased by those local authorities that conspicuously fail to carry out their statutory responsibilities towards the homeless. In 1972 Shelter conducted a nationwide survey on local authorities and published its findings in *The Grief Report*. The survey revealed that there were many discrepancies and shortcomings. The rod which Shelter uses to beat the backs of errant councils is the National Assistance Act of 1948, which laid responsibility for the homeless at their door.

Ironically, this Act declared that 'the existing poor law shall cease to have effect'. The report shows that the workhouses of that era are still in existence in several areas—now used for housing destitute families—and it quotes instances where treatment of the homeless, such as excluding husbands, regulating hours, is not dissimilar from the attitudes of the Poor Law guardians of the last century.

Some families are being treated by local authorities 'in a way that could only be described as punitive, and where their actual rights as citizens appeared to be disregarded'.

The conclusion to be drawn on the evidence of the hundreds of case histories presented in the reports is that 'thousands of "statutorily homeless families" are not recognized as homeless by local authorities and are consequently deprived of their rights under the 1948 Act'.

'In addition, many local authorities positively attempt to transfer their responsibility to another council by sending homeless families to another area,' says the report. It is difficult to imagine a greater contribution to stress in peace time than these examples of local government authorities shrugging off their responsibilities.

When new housing accommodation is being planned the people to be rehoused are never consulted on the type of housing that should be provided by local authorities. Tower blocks are erected and the accommodation allocated to people who have no option but to accept, for there is no alternative. Yet the stress situations created by tower block living are many, and much mental illness results from it. Lynda Lee-Potter, writing in her *Daily Mail* column on 18th October 1972, made this point following a 'battered baby' tragedy. '"How terrible, how wicked, how could she?" we say rightly every time we hear about baby battering cases. Time and time again the mother is living suspended mindlessly and for ever with two, three or four under-fives in a twentieth-floor cell. We put the poor, the inadequate, the people who can never have a voice, into living hells like this.'

If the planners, councillors, architects and builders lived under such conditions themselves they would realize the stressful situations endured by the residents. But they don't.

Employment and retirement

That employment can produce stress situations was recognized in December 1972 by the Greater London Council when it decided that senior officials of the council earning £5,000 a year or more must have sabbatical leave on full pay to relieve the 'stress' of their work. The 'stress' leave of up to three months was to include travelling expenses of up to £250 a year and was designed to safeguard any possible breakdown in health. (The Government's pay policy has for the time being resulted in this decision being 'frozen'.) An extension of the principle to all workers is justified, for many stress situations spring from conditions of employment. Even more important is that an improved system of vocational guidance be introduced. At present both the adult and juvenile employment exchanges exist as job-filling agencies. They pay little or no regard to the existing techniques available to assess the aptitudes and abilities of individuals, and so the majority of people are condemned to work in jobs totally unsuitable for them.

The stress situations that are created by the unjust treatment of women can be lessened by changing the traditional forms of education and upbringing aimed at keeping them subordinate to men. In a society that assesses status in money terms women must be given recognition for any kind of work they do outside the home, within it or both. At the moment the housewife and mother is paid nothing for her services, and the woman worker outside the home gets a lower rate than the male. As long as money values are the yardstick of status, women will feel despised and exploited in these circumstances. The chronic stress response to such a situation can only be nullified by paying the male rate for the job or its equivalent.

At the end of the employee's working life more attention should be paid to the problems of retirement, and to the possibility of transferring older employees to less demanding jobs and of ensuring that those who wish to remain at work after retirement age has been reached can do so by means of projects such as the special workshops of the type pioneered by the Midland firm of Rubery Owen.

Public suspicion of politicians

The harmful effects of environmental stress have already been dealt with. The failure of politicians to restrain abuses of the environment and rising costs has led to the belief that the Government is not working for the benefit of the people but against their interests. This is an irrational belief based on emotion; nevertheless the feeling that politicians are out of touch with the ordinary citizen produces anxiety, and anxiety, as we have seen, damages health. Sarcastic laughter swept across London in December 1972 when the Prime Minister, Mr Heath, discovered that traffic jams occurred in the metropolis and he was forced to walk home. The reaction displayed in letters to the press indicated how out of touch he was with the everyday life of the mass of Londoners. It could have happened equally well to any other leading politician.

We might be more convinced that MPs, and particularly those who make up the government of the day, were truly aware of the stress of living in a big city if they exposed themselves more to the pressures daily endured by Londoners. We might then see the Minister for the Environment living on the perimeter of Heathrow, and the Prime Minister taking up residence at the bottom of Balham Hill, where he would queue every day for an 88 bus to take him to Westminster, inhaling the traffic fumes and experiencing the traffic noise while he waited.

The new killer diseases

Man has subjected himself for hundreds of years to conditions of living which would cause death from the stress response in many wild animals. This indicates his adaptability, but the great increase in stress situations arising from urban industrialized society is now threatening his wellbeing in the way epidemic diseases did a century ago.

The major causes of death at the beginning of this century were influenza, pneumonia, tuberculosis, diphtheria and other wholesale killers.

Public health legislation improved standards of cleanliness and sanitation and dramatically reduced their incidence. In their place have come those diseases in which the body's response to stress plays a major part—among them diseases of the heart and blood vessels, cancerous growths and ulcers of the duodenum and stomach.

The constant over-stimulation of our bodies by the urban environment and by the competitiveness of Western man now has to be controlled in the same way that living conditions were improved by public health measures earlier in the century.

Bibliography

CARGILL, DAVID, *How to Avoid a Coronary Thrombosis.* Hamish Hamilton, London, 1969.

CARRUTHERS, MALCOLM, *The Western Way of Death.* Davis-Poynter, London, 1974.

CONFERENCE OF THE SOCIETY FOR PSYCHOSOMATIC RESEARCH, *The Nature of Stress Disorder.* Hutchinson, London, 1958.

DODGE, DAVID L., and MARTIN, WALTER T., *Social Stress and Chronic Illness.* University of Notre Dame Press, Indiana, 1970.

GORER, GEOFFREY, *Death, Grief and Mourning in Contemporary Britain.* Cresset Press, London, 1965.

KEIRAN, PATRICIA, *How Working Mothers Manage.* Clifton Books, London, 1970.

LEVI, LENNART, *Stress: Sources, Management and Prevention.* Liveright Publishing, New York, 1967.

LEVITT, EUGENE E., *The Psychology of Anxiety.* Staples Press, London, 1968.

MORRIS, SARAH, *Grief.* George Allen and Unwin, London, 1969.

Noise, a Final Report (Chairman, Sir Alan Wilson). HMSO, London, 1963.

NOISE ABATEMENT SOCIETY, *The Law on Noise.* London, 1969.

PETER, L. P., and HULL, R., *The Peter Principle.* Souvenir Press, London, 1969.

Report of the Enquiry into allegations against the Security Forces of Physical Brutality in Northern Ireland (Chairman, Sir Edward Compton). HMSO, London, 1971.

ROSENMAN, R. H., *et al.*, 'Primary Heart Disease in the Western

Collaboration Group Study', *Journal of Chronic Diseases*, vol. 23, New York, 1970.

RYCROFT, CHARLES, *Anxiety and Neurosis*. Allen Lane, the Penguin Press, London, 1968.

SARGANE, WILLIAM, *Battle for the Mind*. Heinemann, London, 1957.

SELYE, HANS, *The Stress of Life*. McGraw Hill, New York, 1956.

Stress, 15 monographs, various authors. Roche Products Limited, London, 1971.

STYPULKOWSKI, Z. F., *Invitation to Moscow*. Thames & Hudson, London, 1951.

TAYLOR, RUPERT, *Noise*. Penguin, London, 1971.

TOFFLER, ALVIN, *Future Shock*. Bodley Head, London, 1970.

TORRIE, MARGARET, *Begin Again: a book for women alone*. Dent, London, 1970.

WOLFF, HAROLD G., *Stress and Disease*. Charles C. Thomas, Springfield, Illinois, 1953.

WOLFF, H. G., WOLF, S. G., and HARE, C. C. (editors), *Life, Stress and Bodily Disease*. Williams and Wilkins, Baltimore, 1950.

WOLFF, S., *Children Under Stress*. Allen Lane, London, 1969.

YUDKIN, SIMON, and HOLME, ANTHEA, *Working Mothers and their Children*. Michael Joseph, London, 1963.

Index